SOMETIMES YOU WIN—
SOMETIMES YOU LEARN

FOR TEENS

Books by Dr. John C. Maxwell
Can Teach You How to Be a REAL Success

Relationships

25 Ways to Win with People

Becoming a Person of Influence

Encouragement Changes Everything

Ethics 101

Everyone Communicates,
Few Connect

The Power of Partnership

Relationships 101

Winning with People

Attitude

Attitude 101

The Difference Maker

Failing Forward

How Successful People Think

Sometimes You Win,
Sometimes You Learn

Success 101

Thinking for a Change

The Winning Attitude

Equipping

The 17 Essential Qualities of
a Team Player

The 17 Indisputable Laws of
Teamwork

Developing the Leaders around You

Equipping 101

Make Today Count

Mentoring 101

My Dream Map

Partners in Prayer

Put Your Dream to the Test

Running with the Giants

Talent Is Never Enough

Today Matters

Your Road Map for Success

Leadership

The 10th Anniversary Edition of the
21 Irrefutable Laws of Leadership

The 21 Indispensable Qualities of a
Leader

The 21 Most Powerful Minutes in a
Leader's Day

The 360 Degree Leader

Developing the Leader within You

The 5 Levels of Leadership

Go for Gold

Good Leaders Ask Great Questions

Leadership 101

Leadership Gold

Leadership Promises for Every Day

Learning from the Giants

— SOMETIMES YOU —
WIN
— SOMETIMES YOU —
LEARN
FOR TEENS

How to Turn a Loss into a Win

JOHN C. MAXWELL

Ⓛ Ⓑ

LITTLE, BROWN AND COMPANY
New York • Boston

The author is represented by Yates & Yates, LLP,
Literary Agency, Orange, California.

Little, Brown and Company

Hachette Book Group
1290 Avenue of the Americas
New York, NY 10104
Visit us at lb-teens.com

Little, Brown and Company is a division of Hachette Book Group, Inc. The Little, Brown name and logo are registered trademarks of the Hachette Book Group, Inc.

The publisher is not responsible for websites (or their content) that are not owned by the publisher.

First edition: February 2015

Library of Congress Cataloging-in-Publication Data

Maxwell, John C., 1947–
Sometimes you win, sometimes you learn for teens : how to turn a loss into a win / John C. Maxwell.
pages cm
ISBN 978-0-316-28409-7 (trade pbk.)—ISBN 978-0-316-28411-0 (ebook)—ISBN 978-0-316-28412-7 (library edition ebook)   1. Failure (Psychology)   2. Learning.   I. Title.
BF575.F14M39 2015
158—dc23

2014035295

Adapted from *Sometimes You Win, Sometimes You Learn* by John C. Maxwell, originally published by Center Street in October 2013

10   9   8   7   6

RRD-C

Printed in the United States of America

To my grandchildren Maddie, Hannah,
John Porter, Ella, and James,

For many years I've wanted to write a book
especially for you as you enter your teen years,
and I've finally done it. As you grow toward
adulthood and experience mistakes, problems,
and failures, remember that everyone loses.
Get up more times than you get knocked down,
and try to learn from every loss. That's how you
turn obstacles into opportunities.
I love you.

Papa

Contents

Acknowledgments

Thank you to:
Charlie Wetzel, my writer;
Stephanie Wetzel, my social media manager
and collaborator on this edition; and
Linda Eggers, my executive assistant.

SOMETIMES YOU WIN—
SOMETIMES YOU LEARN

FOR TEENS

Introduction

Have you ever felt like you weren't allowed to fail? Like your parents and teachers expected you to meet extremely high standards no matter what—even if it didn't seem possible?

Or have you ever lost at something that you wanted to win? Felt stupid when you were wrong? Wished you could have a major "do-over"?

And what happens when you do mess up? Do you feel hopeless, like you can never recover from the mistake?

If your answer to any of these questions is yes, then this book is for you. If you're going to lose—and you are, because everyone does—then why not put a positive spin on it? How do you do that? By learning from it. A loss isn't totally a loss if you learn something from it.

Of course, that's not always easy to do. In a favorite *Peanuts* comic strip, Charlie Brown walks away from Lucy after a baseball game, head down, totally dejected.

"Another ball game lost! Good grief!" Charlie moans. "I get tired of losing. Everything I do, I lose!"

"Look at it this way, Charlie Brown," Lucy replies. "We learn more from losing than we do from winning."

"That makes me the smartest person in the world!" replies Charlie.

Lucy's advice makes a lot of sense, but not everyone learns from his losses. A loss doesn't turn into a lesson unless we work hard to make it so. Losing gives us a chance to learn something, but many people do not seize that opportunity. And when they don't, that's when losing hurts.

It's hard to learn when we're feeling down, because then we have to do things that aren't natural. It's hard to smile when we are not happy. It is difficult to respond with a good attitude when we're numb with defeat. How will we face others when we are humiliated? How do we get back up when we are continually knocked down?

If you really want to become a learner, you need to change the way you look at your losses or mistakes and develop some important qualities that will help you respond to them. I hope this book will be of value to you, teaching you how to learn from your losses. Most of us need someone to help us figure out how to do that.

I believe that by developing the qualities below and

practicing them in your own life, you can learn to move forward from mistakes and use what you learn to grow and succeed:

Humility: The Spirit of Learning
Reality: The Foundation of Learning
Responsibility: The First Step of Learning
Improvement: The Focus of Learning
Hope: The Motivation of Learning
Teachability: The Pathway of Learning
Adversity: The Catalyst for Learning
Problems: Opportunities for Learning
Bad Experiences: The Perspective for Learning
Change: The Price of Learning
Maturity: The Value of Learning

Saint Ignatius Loyola, one of the world's greatest educators, once said that we learn only when we are ready to learn. Emmet Fox, noted twentieth-century spiritual leader, said that difficulties come to you at the right time to help you grow and move forward by overcoming them. "The only real misfortune," he observed, "the only real tragedy, comes when we suffer without learning the lesson."

If you're like most people, you've suffered some loss in your life. Are you ready to learn from it? I hope you'll join me in looking at how you can turn losses into opportunities, and how you can see failures from a different perspective. The ideas in this book can help you now and will continue to do so as you grow into young adulthood. Everybody messes up. You only need to learn how to move on from it.

1

When You're Losing, Everything Hurts

My friend Robert Schuller once asked, "What would you attempt to do if you knew you wouldn't fail?" That's a great question, an inspiring question. When most people hear it, they start dreaming. They are motivated to reach for their goals and to risk more.

I have a question that I think is just as important: what do you learn when you *do* fail?

While people are usually ready to talk about their dreams, they are not as excited to answer a question about their shortcomings. Most people don't like to talk about their mistakes and failures. They don't want to look at their losses. They're embarrassed by them. And you've probably heard someone like your parents, when they mess up, say something corny like, "Sometimes you win, sometimes you lose." The message seems to be, "Hope to win, expect to lose, and live with the results either way."

What's wrong with that? It's not how winners think!

Successful people approach losing differently. They don't try to brush failure under the rug. They don't run away from their losses. Their attitude is never *Sometimes you win, sometimes you lose*. Instead they think, *Sometimes you win, sometimes you **learn***. They understand that life's greatest lessons are gained from our losses—if we approach them the right way.

This One Really Hurt

I've experienced many wins in life, but I've also had more than my share of losses. Some losses came through no fault of my own. However, many were of my own making, coming from bad choices and dumb mistakes. A classic one occurred a few years ago. At that time, I was working on my book *The 17 Indisputable Laws of Teamwork*. About a month before everything was due, I was scheduled to go on a two-week trip. *What a great opportunity to finish writing the book*, I thought. And it was. I can still remember the satisfaction I felt when I finished. It was on the very day I was to return home. With a great sense of completion and fulfillment, I put the manuscript into my briefcase and headed to the airport.

When I arrived, my son-in-law Steve picked me up at the Atlanta airport. He was going to drive us straight to our house in Highlands, North Carolina. But after the long flight, I was hungry, so we stopped to pick up some Mexican food on our way out of Atlanta, and off we went.

As Steve drove, I rode in the passenger seat and got ready to eat, but I managed to drop my fork. I tried to reach down and find it, but it was hopeless. "Steve, pull over, will you?" I finally asked. And Steve, who is used to this sort of thing from me, pulled over to the side of the road so that I could make my search. I got out, started feeling around, and still I couldn't find it. Finally, I moved my briefcase, which was sitting in front of my seat on the floor, and there was the fork. Fantastic! I could finally eat! I climbed back in, and off we went.

About twenty minutes later, after I'd finished my food, I looked over and said, "Where's my briefcase?" That's when it hit me. When I was looking for the fork, I had taken out my briefcase and set it on the side of the road. *And I never put it back in the car!*

The loss of a briefcase would be bad enough, but you have to understand that at the time, when I wrote a book, I wrote everything out by hand with a pen and taped quotes and illustrations right onto the paper. There was no backup until much later in the process. There was only one copy, and all those pages represented months of work. And I had just left all that work on the side of the road.

We had gone twenty miles by the time I realized what I had done. The instant I figured it out, we turned around. And while we were driving back, I was already calling Linda, my assistant. She lived only five miles from that spot, and I knew she could get to it quickly, probably before we did.

A few minutes later my phone rang. I answered with great hope, but my heart sank when she gave me the news that the briefcase was gone! When Steve and I arrived, there was Linda. Sure enough, she was in the right place, but there was no sign of the briefcase. I felt sick. The briefcase and my manuscript were gone!

Over the next several days, I was overwhelmed with emotions. I felt:

- **Stupidity:** I wondered how anyone could be both smart enough to write a book and dumb enough to leave it on the side of the road.
- **Anxiety:** It was hopeless to think I'd ever see my briefcase again, so I spent hours writing down whatever I could remember from the manuscript. After a couple of days, I came to the conclusion that I could rewrite the book, but it would take at least six months. And because I was feeling so low emotionally, I felt certain that it would not be as good as the original.
- **Frustration:** It looked like there was no way to meet my publisher's deadline. I had wasted months of my time. If only I had made a copy. But I hadn't.
- **Despair:** Then I started to doubt myself. *What if I can't rewrite the book at all?* I wondered.

Have you ever lost an important piece of homework? Maybe you couldn't find it in your notebook or backpack. Or you left it at home the day it was due and your mom threw it away. If so, you probably know some of what I felt when I lost my entire book. How could I ever fix this?

While I was feeling discouraged, Linda was undaunted. She started calling local police precincts to see if the briefcase had been turned in to them. On the fourth day, Linda struck gold. The briefcase had been turned in. Better yet, everything was still in it—including the manuscript. We all rejoiced, the book was published, and all was well. However, even to this day, whenever I pick up *The 17 Indisputable Laws of Teamwork* I think of my bad experience and the lessons I learned from it.

Assessing the Loss

The biggest lesson I learned was to create additional copies of my handwritten pages. While I still write everything out by hand, I now fax the completed pages to Linda every night. That way she has a backup in case I ever lose my work again. Which, of course, I hope never to do.

The words *be careful* have been my takeaway from this experience. Mistakes are acceptable as long as the damage isn't too great. Or, as they say in Texas, "It doesn't matter how much milk you spill as long as you don't lose your cow!"

I am convinced that we are all one step away from stupid.

I could have "lost my cow" because of this incident. None of us does life so well that we are far away from doing something dumb. And what has taken a great amount of time to create can be lost in a moment.

Why Losses Hurt So Much

In life, sometimes you win. As a kid, I played basketball and was very competitive. I liked to win, and I hated losing. When I was in my early twenties, I went to a class reunion, where I played in a game against other former players from my high school team. We were all eager to prove we could still play at the same level, and it turned out to be a very physical game. Of course, I wanted to win, so I was very aggressive. After I knocked one opponent to the floor, he shouted in frustration, "Back off, it's only a game!"

My reply: "Then let me win."

I'm not exactly proud of that, but I think it shows how much most of us like to win. When we win, nothing hurts. But when we lose, everything is hard. And the only time you hear someone use the phrase "It's only a game" is when that person is losing.

Think of some of the losses in your life and how they made you feel. Not good, right? And it's not just the pain of the moment that affects us. Our losses also cause us other difficulties. Here are a few:

1. Losses Cause Us to Be Emotionally Stuck

Author and speaker Les Brown says, "The good times we put in our pocket. The hard times we put into our heart." I have found that to be true in my life. In my heart I still carry some of the bad times. I bet you do, too. The negative experiences affect us more deeply than positive ones, and if you're like me, you may get emotionally stuck.

Even after Linda found my briefcase, I kept asking myself how I could have been so stupid. To try to bounce back, I drank a milk shake (comfort food), went swimming, and tried to rest. But no matter what I did, I still continually kicked myself for being so dumb. I felt like a slave to my own moods and feelings.

I usually process through mistakes and failures pretty quickly, but I didn't feel free to do that this time. I was having a very tough time breaking out of my self-imposed prison of what-ifs. I can laugh about it today, but even now I still feel foolish for forgetting something so basic.

It's been said that if an ocean liner could think and feel, it would never leave its dock. It would be afraid of the thousands of huge waves it would have to encounter during its travels. Anxiety and fear can really damage the human heart. So can losses. They can weaken, imprison, paralyze, discourage, and sicken us. To be successful, we need to find ways to get unstuck emotionally.

JOURNAL IT!

Have you ever kept a journal? I've found that many very successful people do. I believe it's because writing in a journal can help you think through your reactions to the things that happen to you. By journaling what you think and feel, you're able to see a situation clearly and figure out what to do next. It allows you to get unstuck emotionally and move forward. I recommend that you keep a journal while reading this book.

For your first journal entry, spend some time writing about your attitude on failure. Many people are really afraid of failure. How much do you fear it? When you do mess up, what feelings get stirred up? Anger? Sadness? Do you feel defeated? How hard is it for you to get unstuck and move forward?

As you continue reading, you'll find more exercises like this one. I also encourage you to write down in your journal how you feel about what you're reading. Doing so will help you to track your progress and growth as you go.

2. Losses Cause Us to Be Mentally Defeated

Life is a series of losses. In childhood you lose your favorite toys. You get older and lose days dedicated to play and exploration. You lose the privilege of being irresponsible and carefree. Later, you'll separate from the protection of your family as you leave the nest and take on adult responsibilities. Over the course of your adult life, you'll lose jobs and positions. Your self-esteem may take a beating. You may lose money. You'll miss opportunities. Friends and family may die or move on. All along, everyone's life is filled with loss. Some losses are great; some are small. And the losses we face affect how we think. Some people handle losing well, while others don't.

Too often losing can go to your head. It can defeat you, and you might have trouble coming up with solutions to your challenges. As the losses build up, they become more of a burden. You probably regret the losses of yesterday. And you fear the losses of tomorrow.

But here's the thing: We want success, but we should train for losses. We need to expect mistakes, failures, and losses in life, since each of us will face many of them. But we need to take them as they come, not allow them to build up. As printer William A. Ward said, "Man, like a bridge, was designed to carry the load of the moment, not the combined weight of a year all at once."

3. Losses Create a Gap between "I Should" and "I Did"

Winning creates a positive cycle in our lives. When we win, we gain confidence. The more confidence we have, the more freedom we'll feel to do what we need to do, even when it's hard. Moving from knowing to acting often brings success.

However, losing can also create a cycle in our lives—a negative one. Losses, especially when they pile up, can lead to insecurity. When we are insecure, we doubt ourselves. Insecurity causes us to hesitate when making decisions. Even if we know what we should do, we are afraid to do it. When such a gap is created and isn't overcome, success becomes nearly impossible.

As I think back on my losses and how they have affected me, I see that there have been times that they made me hesitate. I find that happens to others as well. Here are eleven traps that people tend to fall into when a loss affects their confidence:

- **The Mistake Trap:** "I'm afraid of doing something wrong." Losses hold us back.
- **The Fatigue Trap:** "I'm tired today." Losses wear us out.
- **The Comparison Trap:** "Someone else is better than I am." Losses cause us to feel inferior to others.
- **The Timing Trap:** "This isn't the right time." Losses make us hesitate.
- **The Inspiration Trap:** "I don't feel like doing it right now." Losses demotivate us.
- **The Rationalization Trap:** "Maybe it's really not that important." Losses allow us to lose perspective.

- **The Perfection Trap:** "There's a best way to do it and I have to find it before I start." Losses cause us to question ourselves.
- **The Expectation Trap:** "I thought it would be easy, but it isn't." Losses highlight the difficulties.
- **The Fairness Trap:** "I shouldn't have to be the one to do this." Losses cause us to ask, "Why me?"
- **The Embarrassment Trap:** "If I fail, what will others think?" Losses paralyze us.
- **The Self-Image Trap:** "If I fail at this, it means I am a failure." Losses negatively affect how we see ourselves.

All of these traps are caused by losses, and all of them create the gap between knowing and doing. If we want to be successful, we need to bridge that gap.

> *Which of the traps do you tend to fall into when a loss slows your momentum? What problems do they cause in your life? What would change if you could find a way not to fall into this trap?*

4. The First Loss Often Isn't the Biggest Loss

When we experience a loss, we have a choice. If we immediately respond to it in the right way, the loss becomes smaller to us. However, if we respond the wrong way, or we don't respond at all, that loss becomes greater. And it often leads to other losses. As more losses come at us, they seem to become bigger and bigger, crashing over us like waves in a violent storm. As the number of losses goes up, our self-confidence goes down.

How Do You Talk to Yourself?

Losing can make us compare ourselves to others, but this just makes matters worse, because we rarely do it evenly. We tend to compare our worst to someone else's best. For example, we may compare how we feel on the inside with how someone portrays him- or herself on Facebook. That can lead to a negative cycle of self-talk, meaning the conversation we all have with ourselves in our minds. But there's something you need to know:

The most important person you ever talk to is yourself,
  so be careful what you say.
The most important person that you will evaluate is yourself,
  so be careful what you think.

(Continued)

> *The most important person you will love is yourself,*
>   *so be careful what you do.*
>
>   *With that in mind, make sure you treat yourself kindly and speak positively to yourself. Then you'll be in the right frame of mind to learn and grow, no matter how big the mistake.*

I believe that in times of loss, it's easy to beat ourselves up and focus too much on wishing we could change the past. Our self-talk can become very negative. The more negative it becomes, the larger our losses appear to be to us. If our self-talk is angry, destructive, or guilt producing, we have an even harder time breaking free of the negative cycle. It can be hard, but we need to learn how to move on in a positive way.

5. Losses Never Leave Us the Same

The number or severity of your losses isn't as important as how you experience each of them individually. Yes, all losses hurt. And they make an impact on you, an impact that is rarely positive. Losses change you. But you must not allow them to control you. You can't let the fear of looking silly or getting something wrong paralyze you. You can't let the fear of negative consequences keep you from taking risks.

How do you minimize the negative damage of terrible losses? First, by letting them go emotionally. In 1995, when Jerry Stackhouse was a rookie with the NBA's Philadelphia 76ers, he was asked about his take on life now that he was playing professional basketball. His answer: "Win and forget. Lose and forget." If we want to overcome adversity and keep from being defeated by our losses, we need to get past them. And then we need to learn from them!

Q&A WITH JOHN

Q: What was one of your biggest losses growing up?

A: It was my junior year of high school. I was on the varsity basketball team, and we were expected to do really well. People were saying that we could win the state championship. We just had a lot of talent on the team. But we didn't win the championship. We didn't even come close. It was devastating and discouraging for me, but I learned something big from it. Our team had failed because the juniors and seniors didn't get along. So we didn't work together. What I learned was the importance of teamwork—even more than talent— in winning. The next year, as a senior, I did my part in making us a unified team. And as a result, we played much better— even though the amount of talent was less.

2

Humility: The Spirit of Learning

Have you noticed how easily some people bounce back from losses? They learn from them and become even better than they were before! Meanwhile, others seem to fail, fall, and never get back up again. After they experience something negative, you can actually see the downward spiral starting. It's all down to the spirit of the person. Those who bounce back from losses have a spirit of humility. Because of that, they're more likely to make the changes needed to learn from their mistakes, failures, and losses. They are the opposite of prideful people who are unwilling to let losses be their teacher and as a result fail to learn.

Pride Goes before a Fall

Everyone experiences trouble. Some people are made humble by it. They understand that they're not perfect. Others are made hard. These people refuse to even acknowledge that they've failed or made a mistake. Whichever it is, they carry that spirit with them everywhere they go. For those who allow themselves to become hard, that's tragic, because it's very difficult for a hard person to learn anything.

Ezra Taft Benson, former U.S. secretary of agriculture, observed, "Pride is concerned about who is right. Humility is concerned about what is right." Wouldn't you say that's true? Pride causes people to justify themselves, even when they know they're wrong. And that's just the start! Take a look at the negative impact pride can have on a person:

- **Blame:** Instead of taking responsibility, prideful people blame others. They believe that someone else is at fault whenever things are not working out for them.

- **Denial:** Instead of being objective and realistic, they don't face reality. The prideful person will choose to ignore what is obvious to everyone else and will rationalize his behavior.

- **Closed-Mindedness:** Instead of being open-minded and receptive, prideful people are defensive and opposed to new ideas. They say, "This is the way I've always done it," and they have little interest in anything new.

- **Rigidity:** Instead of being flexible, prideful people are rigid. They say, "We do it my way, or I'm out of here."

- **Insecurity:** Prideful people pat themselves on the back and put down others because they are insecure. They take credit for successes and give others the blame for failures.

- **Isolation:** Instead of staying connected with others, prideful people find themselves out of touch—with themselves, their families, their friends. Pride makes people think it's all about them when really it's all about others.

Do any of those descriptions apply to you? I'm sorry to say that when I was younger, I did not have the humility needed to fill me with the spirit of learning. In fact, I was just the opposite: I was prideful, I was competitive, and I always wanted to win. And when I won, I was obnoxious. If I beat someone, I *told* him I won. And I told everyone he knew that I had won. I put everyone on edge. Worse, I wasn't even aware of it. I didn't realize how prideful I was until some friends gave me the gift of a T-shirt that read, "It's hard to be humble when you're as great as I am." Everyone laughed as they presented it to me, but deep down I suspected they were trying to tell me something.

Later I went to one of my friends and asked if I really was that way.

"Yes," she said, "that's who you are. But we love you and know you can change."

That opened my eyes. Her kind words connected with me and made me feel bad. At that moment, I decided to try to change my attitude from always thinking I was the expert to becoming a learner.

Now, that decision took a long time to implement—two or three years. Arrogant people don't get humble quickly. But it was the beginning of a change in me, a desire to embrace a humility that makes learning possible. I'm still confident, but I work every day to keep that confidence from becoming a barrier to my ability to learn.

You may already be a humble person who possesses the spirit of learning. A humble person is open to the ideas of others and willing to admit when they're wrong. If you are, that's fantastic. But if not, here's the good news: you can change. If I did, then you can, too. If you're not sure where you stand in regard to humility—if your friends haven't given you the T-shirt—then perhaps you need to evaluate yourself. Take a look at the following quiz.[1]

Are You Too Proud?

- *Do you tend to believe you know it all?*
- *Do you tend to think you should be in charge?*
- *Do you sometimes believe the rules don't apply to you?*
- *Do you believe you shouldn't fail?*
- *Do you tend to believe you get things done all by yourself?*

(Continued)

> - *Do you believe you are better than others with less talent or status?*
> - *Do you think you are as important as or more important than others in the group?*
>
> *If you answered yes to many of these questions, you may not have the spirit of learning. Please don't be discouraged. You can change.*

The Good Become the Very Best Due to Humility

People with a lot of talent often perform at a high level, but the greatest—the absolute best of the best—achieve the highest heights because they possess the spirit of humility. I was reminded of this recently when I learned about a story from the early life of one of my heroes: John Wooden. The former UCLA basketball coach is a legend. He won every award in his profession. He was the first person named to the Basketball Hall of Fame as both a player and a coach.[2]

As a young player, Wooden was highly talented—so talented, in fact, that he was in danger of being prideful and unteachable. Growing up, he was always the best player on his team, and he went on to lead his high school team to three state championships. But he was fortunate to learn a lesson early on that helped him to develop a spirit of humility. Wooden explained,

> I had forgotten my uniform and did not want to run the mile or so back to our farm to retrieve it before that afternoon's basketball game. Besides, I was the best player on our team—I was sure there was no way Coach was going to bench me. I was wrong.
>
> When it became clear that I would not be allowed to play without the uniform, I talked a teammate into going home to fetch it for me. After all, I was the star, right? Why shouldn't I be allowed to ask a favor or two from the benchwarmers? With that attitude, it's no wonder that the game started without me in it. When I tried to reason with Coach, pleading with him to let me play because it was clear we were outmatched with our new starting lineup, he told me very simply, "Johnny, there are some things more important than winning."
>
> *Some things more important than winning?* Not many coaches could convince a thirteen-year-old boy to believe that. But as I sat miserably on the bench, watching my team fall farther and farther behind, I started to realize that maybe Coach Warriner was right. Maybe I did need to be taken down a notch or two. As I grew up and that experience stayed with me, I really came to appreciate

its significance. The life lessons in responsibility and humility that I needed to learn trumped a hatch mark in the loss column of a grade school–league record book. And at the start of the second half, Coach let me in the game.[3]

At the age of thirteen, Wooden had all of the qualities arrogant people possess. He thought he was better than others, that he didn't have to play under the same rules as everyone else, that the team couldn't do without him, that he *was* the team. Thankfully, he had a coach who believed there are things more important than winning, such as learning. And fortunately for Wooden, he learned the lesson early in life.

I believe that's one of the key things that made him great. That lesson in humility influenced Wooden in his life and coaching and made him a lifetime learner.

How the Right Spirit Helps You Learn

John Wooden understood that sometimes you win, sometimes you learn—but only when you possess a humble spirit. Humility is the start for all people who learn from their wins and losses. It is a key to success at the highest level.

What? you may be thinking. *I disagree! I can name a dozen people who've achieved big things with arrogant attitudes.* So can I. But what *might* they have achieved had they possessed the spirit of learning? Perhaps they would have been even greater. Humility opens the door to learning and to ever-higher levels of achievement. Here's what it helps us do:

1. Gain a True Perspective of Ourselves and Life

When we are focused too much on ourselves, we lose perspective. We can't see reality except in the ways that it affects *us*. Humility allows us to regain perspective and see the big picture. It makes us realize that while we may be *in* the picture, we are not the *entire* picture.

Humility opens your eyes and broadens your view. Because you aren't focused on justifying yourself or looking good, you have better judgment. Where pride leads to closed-mindedness and always seeks to defend itself, humility allows open-mindedness.

JOURNAL IT!

Do you have an accurate perspective on yourself? Open your journal and write a description of yourself: your personality, positive character traits, and areas where you need to grow. Then ask someone who cares about you to share their description of you. Where do they match? Where do they differ? What can you learn from this other person's outside perspective?

2. Discover How to Grow in the Face of Losses

When you are humble enough to have a clear and realistic view of yourself, your vision is usually also clear and realistic about your mistakes, failures, and other losses. That ability to see things objectively sets you up to learn and grow.

How does a humble person learn from mistakes? By pausing and reflecting. I strongly believe that experience alone isn't the best teacher. Instead, evaluated experience is. Humble people are never afraid to admit they were wrong. When they do, it's like saying they're wiser today than they were yesterday.

JOURNAL IT!

After you admit you've made a mistake, you're free to ask yourself some questions about it. This will set you up to grow from it. Do this by asking:

- What went wrong?
- When did it go wrong?
- Where did it go wrong?
- Why did it go wrong?
- How did I contribute to making it go wrong?
- What can I learn from this experience?
- How will I apply what I've learned in the future?

Try doing this exercise in your journal with a recent mistake you've made.

3. Let Go of Perfection and Keep Trying

My grandson John, the son of my son Joel and his wife, Liz, is a wonderful child. (I'd say that even if he weren't my grandchild!) He's very smart, but he also tends to be a bit serious and a perfectionist. To help him with this, his parents bought him a book entitled *Mistakes That Worked* by Charlotte Foltz Jones. They read through it together, and it helps him to understand that he doesn't need to be perfect to be successful.

One of John's favorite stories in the book is about pharmacist John Pemberton of Atlanta, Georgia. In 1886, the pharmacist wanted to develop a new remedy for prospective customers. He had already invented several items of note and this time he wanted to create a new medicine to relieve exhaustion, aid the nervous, and soothe headaches.

The story goes that Pemberton was happy with his product, a syrup made from coca leaf extract (the main ingredient in cocaine!) that he mixed with water and served chilled. But then, according to the legend, a happy accident occurred. Pemberton's assistant accidentally mixed the concoction with soda water. The drink was transformed. And Pemberton decided not to sell it as a medicine, but instead as a fountain drink. He named it Coca-Cola.[4] Today, Coca-Cola is the most popular soft drink in the world (and no longer contains coca leaf extract). According to the story, success came only when Pemberton admitted that his original vision for the drink was not as good as his assistant's creation.

Novelist Mark Twain was once asked to name the greatest of all inventors. His reply: "Accidents." His answer is clever, but it also reveals a great truth. When we're humble, we are open to seeing our mistakes as possibilities for growth and success.

4. Make the Most Out of Our Mistakes

That brings us to the final way that a humble spirit of learning helps us—by allowing us to make the most out of our mistakes and failures.

When you're competing in the Olympics, there's not a lot of room for error. In events where the times of winners and losers are separated by a fraction of a second, any mistake can cost you the gold. That's what eighteen-year-old slalom skier Mikaela Shiffrin knew going into the 2014 Winter Olympics.

At eighteen, Mikaela was already a veteran competitor in the slalom. Racing since she was very young, she'd already competed at the World Cup level and was the reigning world champion. But this was her first Olympics, and she wanted to win. So when she made a big mistake on her second run, she knew she might have just blown her chance. So did her coach, Roland Pfeifer: "I thought it was over," he said. "That was brutal. I can't describe how it felt. It's over."[5]

In slalom ski racing, competitors travel at high speed down a steep hill covered with "moguls," or mounds of snow. The goal is to zigzag over the moguls and between poles known as "gates" as fast as you can without veering off the course to either side. Skiers have discovered that the fastest way to do that is to always keep your skis in contact with the surface of the snow—not easy when you're flying down a bumpy slope. But whenever a ski leaves the snow, you lose some speed, and your time increases. Plus, you're more likely to lose your balance and veer off-course.

So on that February evening, under the floodlights in Sochi, when Mikaela hit a mogul hard and her outside ski flew crazily off the snow, everyone thought she'd lost her opportunity for a gold medal. But for Mikaela, there was still an outside chance. Why? Because she'd made this same mistake before. Many times, most recently in a competition only weeks prior, where she'd lost a lot of time and placed seventh.

For most people, making the same mistake would lead to the same outcome. But Mikaela Shiffrin is not "most people." Winning was never as important to her as mastery, so she has spent years learning to use her mistakes to improve. Instead of letting this mistake lead to defeat, she drew from previous lessons learned and *used* the mistake to win. She didn't panic. Instead she coached herself: "I said, 'You know what to do—charge back into the course.'"[6] And, speeding through the remaining gates, Mikaela reached the end of the course 0.53 seconds faster than the second-place competitor, taking home the gold.

By learning from her mistakes, with a spirit of humility and a focus on getting better, Mikaela Shiffrin achieved her goal of a gold medal in the Olympics. What goals could you achieve if you follow her lead?

Think about famous people whom you admire for their humility. What do they do to demonstrate it? Which of their traits would you most like to have yourself?

3

Reality: The Foundation of Learning

Charlene Schiff was born into a comfortable, loving family in the small town of Horochow, Poland. She had a good childhood. Her father was a philosophy professor at a nearby university, who loved her and was patient with her, even when she did wrong. Once when her mother was working to paint some rooms in their house, Charlene grabbed the paintbrush and painted the family's piano. Her father didn't yell at her. He did discipline her, but he also took into consideration that she immediately felt bad about what she'd done. And he used the incident to teach her how important it was not to destroy other people's property.

Charlene's mother was a teacher, but she gave up her teaching career to raise Charlene and her older sister, Tia. Her mother doted on her, buying her clothes and toys and encouraging her daily. She had a wonderful life.

An Ugly Reality Emerges

But then things began to change for Charlene. In 1939, when Charlene was ten, Poland was invaded by Germany and the Soviet Union and divided between them. Horochow, where Charlene lived, was annexed by the Soviets. Despite that, life didn't change much for her family at that time. But in 1941 it did. That was when Hitler decided to take over all of Poland and his troops entered the city. Immediately, Charlene's beloved father was dragged off by the Nazis. She never saw him again. Soon Charlene, her mother, and her sister were relocated to a Jewish ghetto and forced to share a single room with three other families. Charlene was only eleven.

Charlene's mother had to do forced labor. And the girls were sometimes made to work as well. There was little food, and it was a struggle to survive. But Charlene's mother came up with a plan. She began looking for people in the country-side who might be willing to take them in and hide them. She found a farmer who agreed to take one of them. It was decided that it would be Charlene's sister, who was five years older than she was. Another farmer said he would take Charlene and her mother.

"One day, in 1942, I guess it was early summer, I don't remember dates, but I remember we got up and I said good-bye to my terrific big sister," recounted Charlene. "Now when we didn't hear for a few days anything, that meant that she arrived in good shape and everything was going according to plan, my mother came home from work and she told me to put on my best clothes and shoes and to take an extra set with me and that we would leave the ghetto that evening."[7]

The ghetto where they were living was bordered on three sides by fences and on the fourth side by a river. Late that night, under the cover of darkness, they left their room and made their way to the river. They waded in. But before they could cross, they heard shots. On the bank of the river, soldiers waited. "We can see you, Jew!" they shouted. Others had the same idea as Charlene and her mother. They also wished to escape. Many who were hiding stood up and raised their hands to surrender. When they did, they were promptly shot.[8]

Charlene and her mother huddled among the reeds. The water was up to the young girl's neck. Her mother kept her quiet and fed her soggy bread. They stayed in the river for four days! But on the morning of the last day, Charlene awoke and her mother was gone. She had no idea where her mother could have gone, or if she was even alive.

A Child All Alone

The reality of her situation was horrible. At age eleven, she was all alone, living in a hostile land where she would be hunted down and killed like an animal. "I felt like screaming but I knew I had to keep quiet," Charlene recalled.[9]

With the soldiers finally gone, Charlene made her way to the farm where they had promised to hide her and her mother.

Instead of a warm welcome, she was told she could spend the day in the barn but that when it got dark she had to leave or the farmer would turn her in to the Nazis.

At first, Charlene couldn't face the reality of her situation. She said, "I lived like an animal, going from forest to forest, in search of my mother. I could not allow myself to think that I would never find my mother. I had to find my mother. Where was I going to go, what was I going to eat, who would take care of me?"[10]

The reality of such an overwhelming situation causes some people to crumble. Instead, Charlene began to adapt and learn what she had to in order to survive. The girl who grew up in town, totally dependent on her mother, learned to survive on her own in the woods. Occasionally she stumbled across other Jewish people hiding from the authorities. Once she came across a small group of men, women, and a baby, who had escaped their ghettos. When the group was discovered by local children, they and Charlene hid in a nearby haystack. But local villagers used pitchforks to jab the haystack, killing all but Charlene.

Another time, when Charlene was returning to her sleeping place after scrounging for food, a girl of about eighteen befriended her and offered to help her. They agreed to meet the next morning. But during the night Charlene had a bad feeling about the girl. The next day, she hid herself high in a tree and waited. Sure enough, the girl showed up, this time with her brother. As Charlene listened, she learned that the two had planned to rob her and turn her over to the authorities for a reward.[11]

Charlene did experience a few moments of kindness during those years. Once, she was discovered sleeping in a barn by a hired farm girl, who brought her food and clothing. "It took a long time to sink in," Charlene remembered. "I had [finally] been treated like a human being, with kindness and generosity. I had forgotten how that felt." The girl fed Charlene for almost two weeks. But then one day two policemen arrived at the farm and shot the farm girl, whom they said was Jewish.[12]

"I spent two years in the woods alone," recounted Charlene. "I slept during the day in a little grave I'd dug, and at night I would crawl out and search for something—anything—to eat. I became very ill."[13]

In 1944, Charlene was discovered by Soviet troops, who literally stepped on her as she lay in her hiding place. They took her to a hospital, where she was slowly nursed back to health. Her goal was to make it to the United States, where other family members had gone before the war. Finally, in 1948, she made the journey there. She had lost her father, mother, and sister. But she had survived.[14]

Build on a Good Foundation

If we want to succeed in life and to learn from our losses, we must be able to face reality and use it to create a foundation for growth. That can be very difficult. People who face horrific experiences, as Charlene Schiff did, can be crushed by them. But even losses less catastrophic than hers can tempt us to avoid reality. We may blame other people for our circumstances. We may rationalize or make excuses.

As much as an escape from reality may give us temporary relief from our problems, the truth is, it's easier to go from failure to success than it is from excuses to success. When we lose sight of reality, we quickly lose our way. We cannot create positive change in our lives if we are confused about what's really happening. You can't improve yourself if you're kidding yourself.

Charlene Schiff used the reality of her situation to learn and grow, becoming resourceful and steadfast. She eventually made her way to America, where she created a life and raised a family. Later, she felt compelled to tell her story so that it would never be forgotten.

Three Realities of Life

Everyone's reality is different. However, there are some realities that are true for all of life.

1. Life Is Difficult

Some people seem to believe that life is supposed to be easy. This is particularly a problem in America today. We expect a smooth, easy road to success. We expect our lives to be hassle free. We expect to get the prize without having to pay the price. That is not reality! Life is hard.

There is no quick and easy way. Nothing worth having in life comes without effort. If we don't understand and accept the truth that life is difficult, then we set ourselves up for failure and we won't learn.

2. Life Is Difficult for Everyone

Even if we are willing to accept that life is difficult for most people, deep down inside many of us secretly hope somehow that this truth won't apply to us. I'm sorry to say it isn't so. No one escapes life's problems, failures, and losses. If we are to make progress, we must do so through life's difficulties. Or as poet Ralph Waldo Emerson stated it, "the walking of Man is falling forwards."

Life isn't easy and it isn't fair. I've had unfair things happen to me. I bet you have, too. I've also made mistakes, made a fool of myself, hurt people I've loved, and experienced crushing disappointments. I bet you have, too. We cannot avoid life's difficulties. We shouldn't even try. Why? Because the people who succeed in life don't try to escape pain, loss, or unfairness. They just learn to face those things, accept them, and move ahead in the face of them. That's my goal. It should also be yours.

Do You Believe This?

How much do you accept the difficulty of life? Ask yourself the following questions:

- *Do you often get frustrated by the unfairness of life?*
- *Do you feel like most people have it easier or better than you do?*
- *Do you believe you would be further ahead if you had gotten more advantages than you've had?*
- *Do you often feel unappreciated or overlooked for recognition?*

If you answered yes to these questions, you may have an unrealistic expectation about life and how easy it should be. It's normal to think that the difficulties you face are unusual and unfair. Recognizing that life is difficult for everyone will help you accept your own situation and figure out how to do well in spite of it.

3. Life Is More Difficult for Some Than for Others

Let's face it: life is more difficult for some than it is for others. The playing field is not level. You may have faced more and greater difficulties in life than I have. You may have faced fewer. Your life right now may feel like clear sailing. Or it may feel like rough waters. And comparing our lives to those of others isn't that productive. Life isn't fair, and we shouldn't expect it to be. The sooner we face that reality, the better able we are going to be to face whatever is coming toward us.

Don't Make Life Harder
for Yourself

Your life is probably plenty difficult already. The reality is that you will have to deal with those difficulties no matter what. One of the keys to winning is to not make things even harder for yourself.

Here are some tips to help you accept reality and avoid making life even more difficult:

1. Keep Growing and Learning

As you know, a lot of people never make the intentional effort to grow. Some think they will grow automatically. Others don't value growth and hope to go forward in life without pursuing it. Still others start off growing, then look at how far they've come and start to level off. It's been said that the greatest enemy of tomorrow's success is today's success. We have to keep moving forward, or else we start moving backward.

2. Think, Think, Think!

People who get ahead think differently from those who don't. They have reasons for doing what they do, and they are continually thinking about what they're doing, why they're doing it, and how they can improve. When life is difficult, don't let your feelings about it get in the way of your thoughts on how to overcome it.

3. Face Reality

Perhaps the people who have the hardest time in life are the ones who refuse to face reality. Author and speaker Denis Waitley says, "Most people spend their entire lives on a fantasy island called 'Someday I'll.'" In other words, they think, *Someday I'll do this. Someday I'll do that. Someday I'll be rich.* They don't live in the world of reality.

If you want to climb the highest mountain, you can't expect to do it overnight. You can't expect to do it unless you've been trained in how to climb and gotten into physical condition. And if you try to deny reality and make the climb anyway, you're going to end up in trouble.

Life is difficult. But here's the good news: many of the things you desire to do in life are reachable—if you are willing to face reality, know your starting place, count the cost of your goal, and put in the work. Don't let your current situation discourage you. Everyone who got where they are started where they were.

4. Be Ready to Adjust

Have you ever heard the expression "cut your losses"? It means to stop doing whatever you had been doing that was causing you to lose. To cut your losses, you have to accept that what you were doing wasn't working, and you have to be willing to adjust to make it better. That's not always easy to do. Instead of cutting our losses, we often rationalize. We try to defend the original decision. We wait to see if it will change and prove us right. But the best thing to do is to face up to a problem and either fix it with a new approach or bail out.

While it's true that acceptance of a problem does not make it go away, acknowledging the reality of a situation will allow you to adjust to any difficulties you might encounter. And that perspective greatly increases your odds of success.

5. Take the Best Action

People who respond correctly to adversity understand that their response to a challenge is what matters. They accept the reality of their situation and then react accordingly. I didn't find that to be easy at first. My natural optimism tends to make me want to ignore a crisis and hope it will go away on its own. That doesn't work. Wishing isn't solving. Denying a problem only makes it worse. So does getting angry and yelling, or taking it out on loved ones. I had to learn to say to myself, "This is the way it is. I have a problem. If I want to solve it, I need to take action. What is the best solution?" When you have a challenge, you can turn your lemons into lemonade, or you can let them sour your whole life. It's your choice.

WHAT CAN YOU DO TODAY?

Open your journal and make a list of all the major challenges you face in life, such as your family situation or a struggle with a subject in school. Next to each challenge, write down a mental or an emotional adjustment you need to make to face it. Then list one action that you can take today to move toward a win in that area.

4

Responsibility: The First Step of Learning

Robert Downey Jr. knows a thing or two about mistakes. Today, the star of *Iron Man*, *The Avengers*, and *Sherlock Holmes* is riding a wave of success. He's rich, he's famous, and the movies he's starred in have earned billions at the box office. But just over a decade ago he was on a much different journey.

In the 1980s and '90s, Downey showed so much promise that he was described as "the best actor of his generation." But behind the scenes, his life was a mess. From the time he was around nine years old, Robert Downey Jr. was a drug addict. And even as he succeeded onscreen, his real-world life was in chaos.

Starting in 1996, Downey's addiction started getting him in trouble with the law. For most of us, being arrested once would get our attention. But even after multiple arrests, multiple trips to rehab, multiple court appearances, and twelve months in prison, Downey stayed on the same destructive path. It looked as if he was going to squander his talent.

Finally, around 2002, after losing yet another major acting job and becoming uninsurable in the film world, he made a decision. He took responsibility for himself. "I just happened to be in a situation the very last time and I said, 'You know what? I don't think I can continue doing this,' " he told Oprah Winfrey in an interview in 2004. "And I reached out for help and I ran with it, you know?"[15]

Today Robert Downey Jr. lives a much different life. He takes responsibility for his actions every day. He stays busy with work. And he practices wing chun, a martial art that he credits with developing discipline in every area of his life. He has also surrounded himself with people who will help him and hold him accountable. When asked about his past, he doesn't deny or minimize it. "To me, here's the only thing: You take responsibility, whether you're outraged by the results or not, that you in some way participate in and create what you're experiencing," he's said. "I don't pretend it didn't happen."[16]

We tend to think of responsibility as something *given* to us by someone who is in a position of authority, such as a parent or a teacher. And that is often the case. But responsibility is also something we must be willing to *take*. And after more than forty years leading and mentoring people, I have come to the conclusion that responsibility is the most important ability that a person can possess. Nothing happens to advance our potential until we step up and say, "I am responsible." If you don't take responsibility, you give up control of your life.

Every time you fail, you have a choice: to take responsibility and do things that lead to future success, or to avoid the temporary pain of responsibility and make excuses. If we respond right to failure by taking responsibility, we can look at our failure and learn from it. As a result, we won't be as prone to making the same mistake again. However, if we bail out on our responsibility, if we don't examine our failures, we don't learn from them. As a result, we often experience the same failures and losses over and over again.

JOURNAL IT!

Some things that happen to us are completely out of our control. But a lot of times, we share at least a tiny bit of the responsibility and we can make a difference in the outcome. In your journal, list things that have happened to you that you feel were someone else's fault. Look carefully at each and see if there was something you could have done to affect the result. Taking responsibility for your part in any situation demonstrates maturity and prepares you for a life of self-sufficiency.

What Happens When We Don't Take Responsibility

People avoid responsibility all the time, especially when they fail or make mistakes. They just don't want to face up to those things. If we do that long enough, a pattern begins to emerge in our lives:

1. We Begin to Feel Sorry for Ourselves

Most of us have allowed ourselves to feel this way at one time or another. Nowadays that sentiment is way too common. But feeling sorry for yourself never allows you to move on and overcome the problem. Feeling sorry for yourself will cause you to focus on what you cannot do instead of what you can do. It is a recipe for continued failure.

2. We Think Life Should Work Differently Than It Does

Life doesn't always work the way we'd like it to. If we had our way, it would be easier. It would be fair. It would be more fun. There'd be no pain and suffering. We would have to work only if we felt like it. And we would never die. But that isn't how life works. Life isn't easy. It's not fair. We do experience pain.

We can get stuck asking why, but seeking an answer to that

question rarely helps. We may never know why unfair things happen. If we focus on the why instead of pushing through the event, we can't make any real progress in our lives.

3. We Start "Blamestorming"

Another pattern that people fall into when they don't take responsibility is what I call "blamestorming." That's the creative process used for finding an appropriate scapegoat.

Any form of blamestorming may be handy in the moment, but it's not helpful in the long run. You can't grow and learn if your focus is on finding someone else to blame instead of looking at your own shortcomings.

4. We Give Up Control

Who is responsible for what happens in your life? Do you believe that your parents are always in control? Do you feel as though your teachers or coaches need to tell you what to do? Or do you take personal responsibility?

Psychologists say that some people possess an *internal* locus of control. This is where they rely on *themselves* for the gains and losses in their lives. Others possess an *external* locus of control, where they blame others when something goes wrong. Which group is more successful? The group that takes personal responsibility. Which people are more content? The group that takes personal responsibility. Which people learn from their mistakes and keep growing and improving? The group that takes personal responsibility.

JOURNAL IT!

Taking responsibility is part of growing up (although not all—even many adults—learn that lesson). Rate yourself on a scale of 1 to 10, where 1 is totally dependent on others and 10 is totally self-reliant. Where are you right now in your life? What actions could you take to have more responsibility for your life? List them in your journal.

Taking responsibility for your life is a choice. That doesn't mean you try to take control of everything in your life. Obviously, you need to live where your parents tell you. You need to listen to your coaches and do your schoolwork. But you can still take responsibility for yourself and every choice that's yours to make.

Abolitionist Henry Ward Beecher said, "God asks no man whether he will accept life. That is not a choice. You must take it. The only choice is how." How will you approach your life? Will you simply allow life to happen to you? Or will you seize the choices you make with enthusiasm and responsibility?

5. We Make Growth and Success Impossible

Real success is a journey. We have to approach it with a long-term mind-set. We have to hang in there, stay focused, and keep moving forward. Excuses are like exits along the road of success that lead us nowhere. Taking the exit is easy, but it gets us off track. It is impossible to go from excuses to success. So we need to get back on the road, keep moving forward. If we want to do something and we take responsibility, we'll find a way. If not, we'll find an excuse. That may take the pressure off of us and make us feel better in the short term, but in the long run it won't make us successful.

What Happens When We Learn to Be Responsible?

In *You Gotta Keep Dancin'*, author and speaker Tim Hansel says, "Pain is inevitable, but misery is optional." A similar thing can be said when it comes to taking responsibility. Losses are inevitable, but excuses are optional. When you move from excuses to responsibility, your life begins to change dramatically. Here's how.

1. You Take Your First Step in Learning

When you take responsibility for yourself, you take responsibility for your learning. The earlier you do this, the better the potential results. If you take responsibility when you're young, you have a better chance of gaining wisdom as you get older. Starting at your age gives you a huge head start.

It's important, though, to take responsibility only for the

things in your life that you can control. You may be tempted to take responsibility for your friends' choices, but those are outside of your control. The only person who can be responsible for your friend's choice is your friend. Likewise, you aren't responsible for the grades your teachers give you; you're responsible only for the work you did to earn them.

Trying to take responsibility for things that are out of your control will only cause you to lose focus, waste energy, and feel discouraged. If you can find the right balance, where you take responsibility for the things you can control and let go of the things you cannot, you will speed up your learning process.

2. You See Things in the Right Perspective

Taking responsibility for yourself does not mean taking yourself too seriously. It also doesn't mean trying or expecting to be perfect. The best learners are people who don't see their losses and failures as permanent. They see them as temporary.

3. You Stop Making the Same Mistakes

What's the major difference between people who succeed and people who don't? It's not failing. Both groups fail. However, the ones who take responsibility for themselves learn from their failures and *do not repeat them.*

If you think about it, how did you learn to walk when you were a baby? You tried something that didn't work and fell down. Then you tried something else that didn't work, and fell down. You probably tried *hundreds* of approaches—maybe thousands—all of which taught you what *didn't* work when it came to walking. And finally, you tried something that *did* work.

That's the way you learned to walk, eat, talk, ride a bike, throw a ball, and all the other basic tasks of growing up. Why would you think you'll ever get to a place where you can learn without failing and making mistakes? If you want to learn more, you need to try more things. But you also need to pay attention to what's *not* working and make adjustments accordingly.

4. You Grow Stronger

Eleanor Roosevelt observed, "You gain strength, courage, and confidence by every experience in which you really stop to look fear in the face. You are able to say to yourself, 'I lived through this horror. I can take the next thing that comes along.'... *You must do the thing you think you cannot do.*"

Every time that you take responsibility, face your fear, and move forward despite experiencing losses, failures, mistakes, and disappointments, you become stronger. And if you keep doing the things you ought to do when you ought to do them, the day will come when you will get to do the things you want to do when you want to do them.

This ability comes only if you take responsibility for becoming the person God created you to be, not someone else. Right now, you're surrounded by friends and peers, and you may feel it's easier to follow the crowd. But remember that you always have to ask yourself: Am I being myself? Am I taking responsibility in this moment? If the answer is no, then it's time for a change. If the answer is yes, then you are becoming stronger day by day.

5. Your Words and Your Behavior Match

The ultimate step in taking responsibility is making sure our actions line up with our words. That's what author and consultant Frances Cole Jones describes in her book *The Wow Factor*. She writes,

> In the Marines, "riggers"—the people who pack (i.e., reassemble after use) parachutes for other Marines—have to make at least one jump a month. Who packed their chute? They do: One of the parachutes that *they* packed for others to use is chosen at random, and the rigger has to "jump it." This system helps make sure that no one gets sloppy—after all, "The chute you're packing may be your own."
>
> The Roman army used a similar technique to make sure bridges and aqueducts were safe: The person who designed the arches had to stand under each arch while the scaffolding was being removed...

Are you performing every task with the concentration and commitment that you might if a life depended on it?[17]

It may sound like overkill when Jones asks if you are taking responsibility for the tasks you perform as if your life depends on it, but it's not really extreme. Why? Because our lives *do* depend on what we do. The life we have is the only life we get here on earth, and it's not a dress rehearsal. Every minute we waste is gone forever. We can either choose to take responsibility for what we do with it, or make excuses.

JOURNAL IT!

Write in your journal a list of times when your words and behavior matched, like when you made a promise to a friend and followed through. Celebrate that you demonstrated responsibility in those situations. Then list situations where you might not have followed through on what you said—such as committing to a task and then not doing it. See which area you fall into more often. What adjustments do you need to make if your actions and words are more frequently inconsistent?

I hope, like me, you are choosing to face reality and take responsibility. If you do that, then you will be ready to dig in and focus on improvement, which is the subject of the next chapter.

5

Improvement: The Focus of Learning

When Gabrielle Douglas stood on the Olympic podium in London, England, in August 2012, she wasn't thinking about how she was the first African-American to win the all-around gold medal in gymnastics. She wasn't thinking about her amazing near-perfect performance that won her the gold. Instead, she was thinking about all the choices she had made in order to improve in the sport, and how in that moment they were all suddenly worth it.

Gabby Douglas showed her talent for gymnastics at a young age—at only four, she taught herself to do one-handed cartwheels. Her sister Arielle noticed and encouraged their mom to sign her up for formal instruction. While training in her hometown of Virginia Beach, Virginia, Gabby advanced quickly. But she sometimes lacked focus, and her nerves often got to her in competition. And then one day, Liang Chow, coach for 2008 Olympian Shawn Johnson, came to Gabby's gym to guest-teach. In an afternoon, he taught Gabby to do an especially difficult vault, and she fell in love with his easygoing coaching style.

Douglas was ready to take her skills to the next level, and she believed Chow was the coach to help her do it. So only two years before the 2012 Olympics, she asked her mother to let her travel to Iowa to train in Liang Chow's gym. She was only fourteen and would be living with a host family that she'd never met, but she and her mother agreed that it was the right decision.

Gabby thrived in the new gym. She focused and worked hard, and Chow challenged her to grow quickly. She said, "Chow definitely brought out the best in me. He pushed me every single day. I remember I was on vault and I kept falling, so I stayed overtime. He came to me and said, 'I have to push you now because if I don't, and if you don't make it, you're not gonna like me because you would have wanted me to push you more.' And ever since that moment, I trusted him. I had to push myself because he was giving one hundred percent so I knew that I couldn't give seventy, I couldn't give ninety—all I could give was one hundred percent back."[18]

But in the young world of gymnastics, Gabby had had a late start. By the time she got to the Olympics, she had competed in only a handful of national and international competitions. Some questioned whether she was ready to perform on this level. One who did was Martha Karolyi, coordinator of the U.S. women's national team. "Physically, yes, she was prepared. We all knew that. But lots of people had a question mark about her ability to focus, and really, this quality has improved in the last five months. She had such a great improvement, it's incredible in such a short time. I haven't seen any gymnast go from an average good gymnast five months ago to climb up to be the best in the world. That's the truth."[19]

Gabby credits the support of her family in helping her overcome nerves and simply do what she did best. Her intense focus on improvement over the two years before the Olympics also played a part. And now, as a one-time Olympic champion, Gabby Douglas is still striving to improve, as she trains for the 2016 Games in Rio de Janeiro, Brazil.

How Do You Respond?

Most of us don't expect to achieve perfection. But we do want to get better and better every day. That requires improvement. And improvement starts with an appropriate response to failure: admitting it. It's been said that the three most difficult words to say are "I was wrong." When we make a mistake or fail, we don't want to admit it. Instead, we often do one of the following:

- **Blow Up:** We react with anger, blame, and rationalization.
- **Cover Up:** We try to hide our mistakes to protect our image.

- **Back Up:** We withdraw from those who might discover our mistake.
- **Give Up:** We throw up our hands and quit.

> *We all make mistakes or fail. When you do, which of the above reactions do you tend to have? How does that reaction help or hurt you?*

Insights on Improvement

Improvement has been a personal passion with me for many years. It's why I'm always reading books and learning from the experiences of others, like Olympian Gabby Douglas. Here are some observations I've made from others' stories and my own experience:

1. When You Improve, Everything Else Gets Better

Success does not always bring growth, but personal growth will always add to our success. The highest reward for our toil is not what we get *for* it but what we become *by* it. The most important question is not "What am I getting?" but "What am I becoming?"

The bottom line is clear. If you are not moving forward, the world is passing you by. If you want to improve your life, your family, your work, your economic situation, your influence, or anything else, you need to first improve yourself.

2. To Improve, You Have to Leave Your Comfort Zone

Novelist Fyodor Dostoyevsky observed, "Taking a new step, uttering a new word, is what [people] fear most." Instead people should most fear the opposite—not taking the step. Why? Because if we don't step forward out of our comfort zone and into the unknown, we will not improve and grow. Staying where it's safe does not take us forward. It doesn't help us to overcome obstacles. You'll never get anywhere interesting if you always do the safe thing. You must give up security to improve. Gabby Douglas gave up almost all of her security when she moved to Liang Chow's gym, which was crucial for her success.

What does it take to get us to move out of our comfort zone? From what I can see, it requires two things:

Don't Fear Mistakes

Getting out of your comfort zone means you're going to make mistakes. Just like a musician trying to learn a new instrument, you find yourself doing things you've never done before. And nobody is perfect at anything the first time they try it. That's why it's important to remember that mistakes are not failures. They are proof that we are making an effort. When we understand that, we can more easily move out of our comfort zone, try something new, and improve.

Don't Let Feelings Control You

Legendary Baltimore Orioles shortstop Cal Ripken Jr. played in more consecutive baseball games than any other player: 2,632 games. That means he didn't miss a single game in more than sixteen seasons! When asked if he ever went to the ballpark with aches and pains, Ripken replied, "Yeah, just about every day."

Ripken didn't allow his feelings—even feelings of physical pain—to overwhelm him or keep him from performing. He pushed through them. If we want to succeed in getting out of our comfort zone so that we can improve, we need to follow his example.

If you want to keep improving, you need to do it even when you don't feel like it. You need to conquer the temptation to give up. Not being controlled by your feelings means that you can face your fears, get out of your comfort zone, and try new things. That is an important part of improvement.

3. Don't Settle for a Quick Fix

A lot of people are looking for quick fixes, because they want the reward without the work. You probably know someone who wants to get into a great college, but doesn't want to study. Or maybe they believe they deserve the lead in the school play even though they've never acted before.

Have you ever heard of "destination disease"? It's the belief that all we need to do is arrive at some goal, and we never have to struggle again. The problem is that life doesn't work that way. If you finish high school with a great GPA, you still have to work once you're in college. Once you turn eighteen, you're a legal adult, but that doesn't mean you can stop learning. Destination disease makes people think they can quit improving at some point, and that makes them search for the quick fix.

Improvement doesn't come to people who focus on quick fixes. It comes to the slow but steady people who keep working at getting better. If you have a quick-fix mind-set, then you need to shift it to continuous improvement. That means doing two things:

Understand That Improvement Is a Never-Ending Battle

I believe all of us can identify with the poet Carl Sandburg, who said, "There is an eagle in me that wants to soar, and there is a hippopotamus in me that wants to wallow in the mud." The key to success is following the impulse to soar more than the desire to wallow. And that is a never-ending struggle—at least it has been for me.

If you are just beginning your improvement journey, don't be discouraged if you're finding it difficult. Your starting point doesn't matter. What matters is where you end up. And you get there by continuing to fight the improvement battle.

Understand That Improvement Is a Result of Small Steps

People today are looking for a secret to success. Look around—most people want a magic bullet, an easy answer, a single thing that will give them fortune or fame. Success generally doesn't work that way. Instead, it comes through small, simple steps in the right direction. That's pretty boring, isn't it? It may not be exciting, but it is true. Small differences over time create a big difference! Improvement happens in inches, not giant leaps.

When I was young, I would see a successful person and say to myself, "I will never be able to achieve that." And I would get discouraged. Why? Because I saw the giant gap between that person and me. The difference between where I was and where that person was seemed impossible to overcome.

Have you ever felt that way? Do you look at students who are ahead of you in a subject and think you could never be like them? If you like to draw or paint, do you look at the great masters and get discouraged because they're so much better than you? What we all need to realize is that the way those people got where they ended up was through small steps—small victories, little sacrifices, simple choices to work hard in the moment. We may only see the results, but the steps were taken, even if they're hidden.

4. Commit to Daily Improvement

Fairly early in my personal growth journey, I heard something from Earl Nightingale, a great speaker and author, that changed my life. He said, "If you study a subject every day for one hour a day, five days a week, in five years you will become an expert in that area." Can you imagine? Think of the areas where we all could become experts! Five years may feel like a long time, but they're going to go by no matter what you do. Wouldn't it be great if you could be an expert in something by then?

Some things simply have to be done every day. You know the old saying, "An apple a day keeps the doctor away"? Well, eating seven apples all at once isn't going to give you the same benefit. If you want to improve, you need to make growth a habit. A habit is something you do continually, not once in a while. Feelings of excitement may get you going, but the positive habits you develop and practice consistently are what keep you improving.

As I have worked to improve every day, two words have helped me to stay on track:

Intention

Every morning as I start my day, I *intend* to learn something that day. This makes me look every day for things that will help me improve.

Contemplation

Time alone to think is so important for self-improvement. When you spend time thinking about your experiences, it helps you see bad experiences in a different light. You can actually evaluate losses and learn from them. Contemplation time by yourself also allows you to do positive self-talk, where you tell yourself what's good about your situation. During your "conversations" with yourself, you can beat yourself up and make yourself feel really small, or you can learn and build yourself up so that you become better.

JOURNAL IT!

Do you spend time alone just thinking? Nowadays, most people fill their alone time with the Internet or their phones. I encourage you to put your phone down and spend time thinking! And if you're not sure what to think about, ask yourself the questions that I ask myself at the end of every day:

(Continued)

- What did I learn today? What spoke both to my heart and my head?
- How did I grow today? What touched my heart and affected my actions?
- What will I do differently? What small steps can I take to improve?

Ask yourself these questions every day and record your answers in your journal to track your growth over time.

One thing you shouldn't do during your thinking time is compare yourself to others. When you want to truly improve, it's about being better than you used to be, not better than some other person. Intention and contemplation will help you do that.

Make Improvement Intentional

Improvement is within the reach of anyone, no matter how old or young, educated or ignorant, rich or poor. To start improving today, do these three things:

1. Decide You Are Worth Improving

Author Denis Waitley has a wonderful definition for personal development. "Personal development," he says, "is the belief that you are worth the effort, time, and energy needed to develop yourself. It gives you permission to invest in yourself so you can develop your own potential."

Your dreams are worth investing in. You don't need anyone's dreams but your own. And you don't need to become anyone other than yourself at your best. The great philosopher Thomas Carlyle once wrote, "Let each become all that he was created capable of being." I can't think of a better definition of success. In life, you'll face challenges every day. You can consider yourself a success when you reach for the highest that's within you—when you give the best that you have. Life doesn't require you to always come out on top. It asks only that you do your best to improve at whatever level of experience you are currently on.

JOURNAL IT!

In your journal, list ten reasons why you are worth improving. If you can't come up with ten, ask someone who cares about you to help you make the list.

---

2. Pick an Area to Improve

Most people either want to improve nothing, or are so impatient to grow that they try to improve everything at the same time. Those are both mistakes. You need to focus.

Think about your life right now: your classes at school, your friendships, your extracurricular activities. Are there one or two areas within those categories that you'd like to improve? Focus on spending time each day improving in those areas. You may not see a difference in a day or a week, but you will over time. You'll be amazed by how much you can get done in a year. We always overestimate what we can get done in a day or a week. But we underestimate what we can get done in a year. Just imagine how much you can grow in twelve months if you do a little every day!

3. Figure Out How a Loss Can Help You Improve

Improving a little every day is important to success. But so is learning from your losses as they come. Some lessons in life cannot wait. So you need to make the most of them when they happen. If you don't look at what went wrong while the details are fresh, you may lose the chance to learn the lesson. And if you don't learn the lesson immediately, you may experience the loss again!

Have you ever given a presentation in front of your class and lost your train of thought? Or been on a team that just lost a game? In those moments following the failure, you might want to shut down or think about something else. But if you take the time to figure out what went wrong, you can start to learn and improve from your mistakes.

I always try to remember that I am a work in progress. When I look at things that way, I realize that I don't have to be perfect. I don't have to have it all together. I don't need to try to have all the answers. And I don't need to learn everything in a day. When I make a mistake, it's not because I'm a failure or worthless. I just didn't do something right because I still haven't improved enough in some part of the process. And that motivates me to keep growing and improving. If I don't know something, it's an opportunity to try to improve in a new area. I'm in it for the long haul.

6

Hope: The Motivation
of Learning

It's been over a decade since surfer Bethany Hamilton was attacked by a shark off the coast of the island of Kauai, in Hawaii. You may know her story. In October 2003, when she was thirteen years old, she lost her left arm up to the shoulder to a fourteen-foot tiger shark. At that time she was already a champion amateur surfer. But surfing was more than just a hobby for Bethany; it was her career goal. She'd been competing since age eight and had every intention of going pro. But after such a catastrophic incident, how could anyone hope to make surfing a career?

Bethany was injured on a Thursday, and as soon as she and her family learned that she would survive, everyone immediately thought of how it would affect her ability to surf. Losing her arm made Bethany and those around her assume she could no longer pursue her goal of becoming a pro surfer. They talked about alternative careers, like surf photography.

And they seriously discussed those other options—for two whole days.

"By Saturday," Bethany says, "I changed my mind and started thinking about going surfing again."[20] She refused to abandon her dream, and she was eager to try to surf under her new circumstances.

Everyone knows that you need two arms to surf. Surfers paddle out from the beach with strong strokes from both arms. They dive under breaking waves on their way out, grabbing the board by the "rails," or the two sides. Then when they've dropped into the wave and it's time to get up, they grab the rails again and push up to a standing position. With only one arm, how was Bethany going to paddle out, or dive, or stand up?

But Bethany's hope only grew stronger. Her doctors insisted that she stay out of the water until her stitches came out. As soon as they did—less than a month after the accident—she and her dad went surfing.

"I told myself, 'You can do it,'" she writes in her book, *Soul Surfer*. "'You can paddle and get up with one arm.' But quickly another voice inside my head yelled back, 'Forget it. You're going to fail.' I tuned out that nagging self-doubt and headed for the water."[21]

At first, she struggled. She had a hard time holding on to her board. Then, when she did get up, the board shot out from under her. But on only her third wave, she figured it out. Her dad describes it: "Bethany looked over at me. For a moment, our eyes met. That's when I saw it. That flash of fire. It was still there. The wave rose up behind us, ready to break. Bethany leapt to her feet. She caught it perfectly. I watched her ride the wave all the way to the distant shore."[22]

Bethany often has to tell people she doesn't paddle in a circle just because she has only one hand.[23] Using her strong right arm and her feet to propel her, she paddles out as straight as she did before. To make it easier for her to dive under the waves, her dad installs handles in the center of her boards for her to hold on to. And she's become an expert at planting her right hand in the center of the board to push up to a standing position.

Today, Bethany says she feels like she's known as "that surfer girl that lost her arm," but that many don't know that she still surfs, or how good she really is.[24] She got the hang of surfing with one arm very quickly, and she was competing again within only three months of the accident. She won a major competition in 2005, turned pro in 2007, and has continued to compete ever since, often placing in the finals and in 2014 winning the Surf n Sea Pipeline Pro.

Surfing was never replaced in her life with another career, but Bethany's accident did lead to some additional opportunities that she would never have dreamed of. She wrote the book *Soul Surfer*, and Hollywood made a movie of the same name that told her story. She's also in demand as an inspirational speaker. And her charity, Friends of Bethany, has the mission to "support shark attack survivors and amputees, worldwide; and present inspiring life stories through movies, projects, and activities."[25]

Bethany is currently working on another movie—this time a documentary showing her surfing some of the most beautiful surf spots in the world. And she has a new book: *Body and Soul: A Girl's Guide to a Fit, Fun, and Fabulous Life*.

Bethany Hamilton's belief in herself might have wavered for a day or two, but now hope is what sustains her as she faces every challenge of life. As she says, "Whatever your situation might be, set your mind to whatever you want to do and put a good attitude in it and I believe that you can succeed. You are not going to get anywhere just sitting on your butt and moping around."[26]

Hope Is a Beautiful Thing

Losses in life are never fun, but there is one loss no one can afford to experience—the loss of hope. If you lose hope, that may be your last loss, because when hope is gone, so is motivation and the ability to learn. Hope gives. It gives to us even when we have little or nothing left. It is one of the most precious things we have in life.

Hope is inspiring. It gives us the motivation for living and learning. I say that for several reasons:

1. Hope Says Yes to Life

Where does a person find the courage to say yes to life? I believe it comes from hope. Life isn't always rosy. In life, we all experience trouble. We go through hard times. We experience conflict. But those facts don't mean you have to lose hope. You can be encouraged by Bethany Hamilton: "You can and will get through it. I'm living proof that when there's a will, there's a way."

2. Hope Fills Us with Energy

It's been said that a person can live forty days without food, four days without water, four minutes without air, but only four seconds without hope. Why? Hope provides the power that energizes us with life. Hope is a powerful thing. It keeps us going when times are tough. It creates excitement in us for the future. It gives us reasons to live. It gives us strength and courage.

3. Hope Focuses Forward

Our yesterdays have a tendency to invade our todays with negative feelings, stealing our joy and hope. If we dwell on them too much, they threaten to rob us of our future. That's why I like these words of Ralph Waldo Emerson: "Finish each day and be done with it.... You have done what you could; some blunders and absurdities no doubt crept in; forget them as soon as you can. Tomorrow is a new day; you shall begin it well and serenely."

Hope always has a future. It leans forward with expectation. It wants to plan for tomorrow. And that opens us up to greater possibilities.

4. Hope Is a Difference Maker

Recently I read *No Ordinary Times*, a biography of Franklin and Eleanor Roosevelt during World War II, written by Doris Kearns Goodwin. Many pages of the book were dedicated to England and Prime Minister Winston Churchill's leadership during the dark days of World War II.

Churchill certainly was a leader of hope to his people. As the Nazis swept across Europe and then rained down bombs on England during the Blitz, the task of defeating Hitler and the Nazis seemed impossible. Yet, despite the odds against them, the British stood firm.

How was one relatively small nation, standing alone for quite a long time, able to stand up to the Nazis? When Winston Churchill was asked what was England's greatest weapon versus the Nazis, he responded with one word: *hope*.

Hope is the greatest weapon we can use to battle our losses when they seem to be growing. It is powerful, and that is why I call it a difference maker.

What Does Hope Do for Us?

- *Hope looks for the lesson in defeat instead of just leaving you feeling defeated.*
- *Hope discovers what can be done instead of what can't be done.*
- *Hope regards problems, small or little, as opportunities.*
- *Hope lights a candle instead of cursing the darkness.*
- *Hope opens doors where despair closes them.*
- *Hope draws its strength from what can be instead of what was.*
- *Hope cherishes no illusions nor does it yield to cynicism.*
- *With hope, failure is a skipping stone. Without hope, failure is a tombstone.*

How to Cultivate Hope

Since hope is such a beautiful thing, this question has to be asked: "Can anyone have it?" The answer is yes! Regardless of your present situation, background, personality, upbringing, or circumstances, you can be a person of hope. Doing the following three things will help you to get there.

1. Choose Hope

Hope is deep inside of men and women who learn from their losses. When times are tough, they choose hope, knowing that it will motivate them to learn and turn them from victims into victors.

Some people say choosing hope is a pie-in-the-sky approach to life. It's unrealistic, they claim. I disagree. In *The Dignity of Difference*, Jonathan Sacks writes, "One of the most important distinctions I have learned...is the difference between *optimism* and *hope*. Optimism is the belief that things will get better. Hope is the faith that, together, we can make things better. Optimism is a passive virtue, hope an active one. It takes no courage to be an optimist, but it takes a great deal of courage to have hope."[27]

JOURNAL IT!

Hope is a choice. It's not a feeling that comes over us. One good way to make that choice is to examine all the reasons why we should have hope. Maybe you have skills that you can use in a career. Or you have people in your life who love you. Take some time to list in your journal all the reasons you can think of for choosing hope. Then choose to have hope, believing that it will yield good results.

I believe everyone is capable of choosing hope. Does it take courage? Yes. Because hope can be disappointing. But I am convinced that the courage of choosing hope is always rewarded.

2. Change Your Thinking

In general we get what we expect in life. I don't know why that is true, but it is. If your expectations for life are negative, you end up experiencing a lot of negative events. And consequently, with every negative experience, your expectations become more negative for the future. This is especially painful, because negative expectations cause a person to not learn from their losses.

The good news is that you don't have to live with negative thinking. You can change your thinking from a negative mind-set, in which you feel hopeless, don't learn from your losses, and are tempted to give up, to a positive mind-set, in which you believe things can get better, you learn from your mistakes, and you never quit.

As I said, it's simple but it's not easy. If you have been a negative thinker who doesn't see life through the eyes of hope, then you must make a choice every day to try to renew your hope, change your thinking for the better, and believe that good things can and will happen to you. Doing these things can literally change your life.

3. Win Some Small Victories

If you are able to develop your hope and become more positive in your thinking, that's a great start. But it's not enough. Positive thinking must be followed by positive doing. If you want to succeed big, then start by trying for a small victory. Nothing encourages hope like success.

If you are able to win small victories, it encourages you. It affects your attitude. When you experience a win once, you begin to understand how it works. You get better at succeeding, and after winning several victories you begin to sense that bigger victories are nearly within your grasp. Maybe your small victory will be eating lunch with someone outside your usual group of friends, and you discover a new friend who has a lot in common with you. Or you'll work hard and raise a C grade to a B. Or perhaps you'll work hard enough in sports practice that the coach notices and compliments you. Even a small improvement or victory can give hope. And hope is a powerful motivation for continued change and learning.

Q&A WITH JOHN

Q: If I'm not very good in school, how do I have any hope that I can learn and grow, like you're teaching in this book?

(Continued)

A: The first thing to understand is that there's more than one kind of smart. (A great book on this is *7 Kinds of Smart*, by Thomas Armstrong.) Academic success uses only one kind. If you've been discouraged in school, you need to change your thinking and recognize that you have something else to offer. Whether you're good with people, or with your hands, or in athletics, or artistically, focus on growing in that area. Too many people focus all their attention on improving their weaknesses. But you can still try to do your best in school and devote lots of energy to growing in your strengths.

The Power of Hope

Jim Abbott was born without a right hand. His parents, Mike and Kathy, sought answers for the birth defect. So did Jim's doctors. But they never found a specific reason for it. It was something that had merely happened, and the young parents had to find a way to deal with it.

Jim played like a normal kid, and he didn't seem to be slowed down too much by the absence of a hand, but when he got to be five, the experts advised Mike and Kathy to have him fitted with a prosthesis and be trained to use it. Back in those days, that meant a hook.

Jim's parents followed the advice, and Jim did receive a hook and learned to use it. He worked at it alongside kids with severe disabilities, such as a child who was learning to brush her teeth with her feet because she had no arms. But there came a moment in the hospital when they realized that Jim didn't really belong there. They knew their best hope would be to treat him as a normal kid. Jim's parents removed him from the hospital and took him home.

During the drive home, Mike told Kathy, "We don't have a problem. We've got a blip on the screen. We can handle this. We could make it a problem if we want it to be a problem. But, it's no problem anymore."[28] Jim writes, "On that two-hour trip [going home from the children's hospital], we'd get our strength back. Mom and Dad felt hope, even optimism, for the first time beginning to focus not on what I lacked but what I had."[29]

Two of the things Jim had were a love for sports and good athletic ability. When Jim was six, his father bought him a baseball glove. He loved it. He spent hours throwing a rubber baseball at a brick wall, improving his aim and arm strength, and figuring out how to get his glove from his right arm onto his left hand so that he could field the ball when it bounced back. Once he came up with a system, he kept getting faster and more smooth. As he got better, he stood closer to the wall so that he had to make the switch more quickly to catch the ball.

Baseball wasn't Jim's only love. He played every sport. He'd go out with the neighborhood boys and be part of every pickup game. At first, nobody would pick him. There were times when he came home discouraged and wanted to give up. But his dad wouldn't allow it. Mike would send his son back out to the playground to keep trying. He had hope for Jim and wanted him to learn to persevere and overcome obstacles. He was preparing him for the road ahead.

Jim says, "The thing about a disability is, it's forever."[30] It's not going away, so you have to learn how to deal with it. How did Jim do that? He played every sport and did everything he could to improve himself. And he started to get some recognition, because he was good—so good, in fact, that he dreamed of someday playing baseball professionally, a goal he shared for the first time with friends and family when he was twelve. "It seemed like a lot to hope for, but I had plenty of hope, and plenty of help," Jim explains.[31]

Hope Pays Off

"I was no prodigy. I was cut from the freshman basketball team at Flint Central High School. I made the freshman baseball team, but didn't get a hit the whole season. It was a long time before I separated myself from boys my age on athletic fields," says Jim.[32] But separate himself he did. As a high school sophomore, he played varsity baseball. When he was a junior, the coach told him he was the ace. Jim batted .367 that year and helped his team become city champions.

That year his coach also recruited him to play football as the backup quarterback. He was reluctant, but his coach insisted. Jim ended up starting in the playoffs and nearly took the team to a state championship.

As a senior, Jim played first base, pitched (winning ten games with an ERA of 0.76), and batted cleanup (.427 average). His team won the conference championship, and the Toronto Blue Jays drafted him. But Jim had his heart set on playing for the University of Michigan, which he did for three years. He was an All-American, winning two Big Ten championships. And he played on the Olympic baseball team. He pitched the gold-medal game in the 1988 Summer Olympics in Seoul, South Korea.

Jim's dream came true when he was again drafted, this time by the California Angels. He was the eighth pick of the 1988 draft. He expected to spend a long time in the minors, working his way up. But much to his surprise, he made the major league roster on opening day of his first year.

Hope Pays Back

Jim played major league baseball for ten years. Some seasons he was fantastic. Other years he struggled. A particular highlight of his professional career was the no-hitter he pitched in 1993 at Yankee Stadium. There were many things about playing major league baseball that he misjudged or didn't expect. But the thing that turned out to surprise him the most was the attention he got from children with disabilities similar to his.

Jim remembered what a thrill it was for him to meet a major league ballplayer, so the fact that kids would want to talk to him or get his autograph wasn't a surprise. But he didn't expect parents and their physically challenged kids to seek him out as they did. Jim writes,

> I didn't see them coming, not in the numbers they did. I didn't expect the stories they told, or the distance they traveled to tell them, or the desperation revealed in them.
>
> They were shy and beautiful, and they were loud and funny, and they were, like me, somehow imperfectly built. And, like me, they had parents nearby, parents who willed themselves to believe that this accident of circumstance or nature was not a life sentence, and that the spirits inside these tiny bodies were greater than the sums of their hands and feet.[33]

Jim says he never turned down a single child, even when he was exhausted or discouraged or busy. Why? He wanted to give them hope! He wanted them to understand that so much was possible for them. Jim says, "I knew these kids and I knew how far a little boy or girl could run with fifty words of reassurance."[34]

Jim retired from baseball in 1999. In his career he pitched 1,674 innings, struck out 888 batters, and won 87 games.[35] He had lived out a dream, one that few people would have thought possible. He gave himself to baseball, and baseball gave him a lot in return. Jim sums up, "Maybe the greatest gift [from baseball] was that it helped me come to peace with the burden of being different." But he also points out, "The lesson had to be learned through losing, painful as it was."[36]

How was Jim Abbott able to learn from his losses? Because he had hope. He kept believing, and he kept trying. Hope provided the motivation for learning. And he used that motivation to learn more and go further than others believed was possible. That is the power of hope.

7

Teachability: The Pathway of Learning

Josh Waitzkin started playing chess at age five. It wasn't long before he was described as a natural. He soon began winning scholastic chess championships around the world. His aggressive style and ability to pull victory from defeat got people's attention throughout his childhood. His dad even wrote a book about Josh's early chess experiences called *Searching for Bobby Fischer*, which went on to become a movie. And nothing could have prepared Josh for the attention he'd receive when the movie hit theaters. He was sixteen, and it nearly ruined his life.

The movie made Josh a star, but the celebrity status distracted him and made it hard to play chess. He couldn't focus anymore, surrounded by crowds of autograph seekers. He became more worried about what others thought. And worst of all, it sucked the joy out of the game. After only a few years, Josh abandoned competition.

His story might have ended there, with a prodigy who

flamed out. But in his early twenties Josh started training in a martial art called Tai Chi Chuan, also known as Push Hands. He loved getting to start as a beginner. He writes in his book *The Art of Learning*, "Given the complicated nature of my chess life, it was beautifully liberating to be learning in an environment in which I was simply one of the beginners."[37]

He started as a beginner, but he didn't stay a novice for long; within two years, he was winning championships. He won an unprecedented total of five National Championship titles in the Middleweight, Light Heavyweight, and Heavy-weight divisions. His biggest victory occurred in 2004 in Taiwan, the birthplace of Tai Chi Chuan, where he won the Middleweight World Championship title in Fixed Step Push Hands and became the Middleweight World Co-Champion in Moving Step Push Hands.[38]

What made Josh Waitzkin a champion again, in an activity totally different from chess? He was teachable. "What I have realized," he writes, "is that what I am best at is not Tai Chi, and it is not chess—what I am best at is the art of learning."[39]

Humble and open, Josh was willing to make mistakes, to look like a novice to his teacher, William Chen, and to admit when he was wrong. He says that wasn't always the case with his fellow students. "When Chen made suggestions, they would explain their thinking," he writes, "in an attempt to justify themselves. They were locked up by the need to be correct."[40] Josh wanted to learn more than to be right.

Josh wrote his book in an attempt to examine how his

learning style had worked for him, and to teach others how to apply it to their lives. Today he works as a consultant and performance coach, teaching people how to learn. He founded the JW Foundation and the Art of Learning Project. And he took up Brazilian Jiu Jitsu, rising once again in the ranks of students to become a black belt.

Teachability Makes the Difference

People often ask me what most determines if they will reach their potential. My answer: a teachable spirit.

What does it mean to be teachable? I define teachable people as those who make the choice to learn and grow throughout life. Some people don't do that. Jazz trumpeter and bandleader Louis Armstrong described them when he said, "There are some people that if they don't know, you can't tell them." Some people want to be right, even when they aren't. And as a result, life is difficult for them. They never find the pathway of learning, nor do they learn the lessons life offers to those with a teachable spirit.

It's easier to be teachable when you know you're not good at something. But what about areas where you have talent? You may do something really well, but that doesn't mean you can't improve. In order to truly live up to your potential, you have to be open to learning. You have to have a teachable spirit.

If you want to be successful tomorrow, then you must be

teachable today. What got you to where you are won't keep you here. And it certainly won't take you where you want to go. You need more than a great mind for learning. You need to have a great *heart* for learning. That's what a teachable spirit gives you.

Traits of a Teachable Person

So, how can you become a teachable person? By developing the following five traits, you'll be on a path to success:

1. Teachable People Have a Positive Attitude toward Learning

People with a teachable spirit approach each day as an opportunity for another learning experience. Their hearts are open. Their minds are alert for something new. Their attitudes are expectant. They know that success has less to do with having natural talent and more to do with choosing to learn.

When you were younger, your parents, teachers, and the school took primary responsibility for your learning. They told you how and when to study. But as you've gotten older, you've been placed more and more in charge of your own learning. Now you decide when and how—and if—you study. And at this stage of your life, a dividing line starts to appear between those who stay teachable and those who resist learning. The choices you make during this time are significant.

You can choose to remain teachable and fuel an internal desire to keep growing. Or you can start avoiding learning opportunities.

Being teachable depends on two things: capacity and attitude. Capacity is our natural ability to learn, and it may to some degree be set. But our attitude is totally our choice. You have to *decide* to keep an attitude of teachability. At Harvard and other universities, they studied the importance of attitude to people's success. And attitude was found to be far more important than intelligence, education, special talent, or luck. In fact, the researchers concluded that up to 85 percent of success in life is due to having a positive, teachable attitude, while only 15 percent is due to ability.[41]

I've known very few teachable people whose approach toward life was negative. Most people with a teachable spirit and positive attitude don't allow negative ideas to hijack their thinking. Why? A closed mind does not open doors of opportunity. A negative attitude rarely creates positive change.

If you have not developed a positive attitude and teachable spirit, I encourage you to fight for them. The sooner you do it, the better, because as age increases, your negative thoughts, bad habits, and weak character traits become more permanently set. Getting older doesn't mean getting better. It just means you have less time to make the choice to become teachable. So choose it now. I know of no other way to keep learning in life.

2. Teachable People Have A Beginner's Mind-set

Successful people are continually learning new things. What's the best way to do that? Have a beginner's mind-set. Erwin G. Hall observed, "An open mind is the beginning of self-discovery and growth. We can't learn anything new until we can admit that we don't already know everything." If you want to grow and learn, you must approach as many things as you can as a beginner, not an expert.

What do all beginners have in common? They know they don't know it all, and that shapes the way they approach things. In general, they're open and humble, without an attitude of "been there, done that." When you were very young, you had a beginner's mind-set in every area. You eagerly learned how to walk, and talk, and read, and count. The possibilities were almost endless. As Zen master Shunryu Suzuki wrote, "In the beginner's mind there are many possibilities, in the expert's mind there are few."

Most of us enjoy being experts. In fact, some people enjoy it so much and feel so uncomfortable as beginners that they work hard to avoid trying to learn anything new. They decide they're satisfied with what they already know. But that attitude may make the difference later in life between, for example, an average singer and a professional one. It's a challenge to stay open in every circumstance and situation over the course of time, but it's worth it.

I try to maintain a beginner's mind-set in all things, even though it's often difficult. To help me do it, I like to keep the following three philosophies in mind:

1. Everyone has something to teach me.
2. Every day I have something to learn.
3. Every time I learn something, I benefit.

Do You Have a Beginner's Mind-set?

Answer yes or no to the following statements:

- *I always enjoy the first day of class in school.*
- *It doesn't bother me when I'm not the expert.*
- *When I face a new challenge, I look forward to solving it.*
- *I see problems as a chance to learn something new.*
- *I love to try new things, like hobbies, activities, school subjects, etc.*

If you answered yes to most of these, you probably already have a beginner's mind-set. If you answered no to some, then you may need to focus on growing in those areas.

---

3. Teachable People Are Willing to Take Long, Hard Looks in the Mirror

Novelist James Thom remarked, "Probably the most honest, 'self-made' man ever was the one we heard say: 'I got to the top the hard way—fighting my own laziness and ignorance every step of the way.'" Can you relate to that statement? I certainly can. I'm known for writing and speaking on leadership, but the most difficult person I have ever led is me!

Becoming and remaining teachable requires you to honestly and openly evaluate yourself on a continual basis. Anytime you face a challenge, loss, or problem, one of the first things you need to ask yourself is "Am I the cause?" This is a key to teachability. If the answer is yes, then you need to be ready to make changes.

When people refuse to look in the mirror and instead look to other people or situations to blame, they keep getting the same result over and over. Recognizing your own part in your failings, seeking solutions (no matter how painful), and working hard to put them into place is teachability in action. And it leads to the ability to change, grow, and move forward in life.

4. Teachable People Listen When Others Speak into Their Lives

One day a fox, a wolf, and a bear went hunting together. After each of them caught a deer, they discussed how to divide the spoils.

88

The bear asked the wolf how he thought it should be done. The wolf said everyone should get one deer. Suddenly the bear ate the wolf.

Then the bear asked the fox how he proposed to divvy things up. The fox offered the bear his deer and then said the bear ought to take the wolf's deer as well.

"Where did you get such wisdom?" asked the bear.

"From the wolf," replied the fox.

Unfortunately, most of us are too much like the bear. We don't like it when people speak the truth into our lives, and when someone has courage enough to speak up, we attack them. We need to react differently.

Think of the people you surround yourself with: your friends, teammates, mentors, and teachers. Do you have anyone in your life who knows you really well and is willing to tell you the truth, even if you don't really want to hear it? To be teachable, you need to have those people around you. Then when they do share feedback and criticism, you have to accept it without attacking them. Otherwise, they'll never share it again!

I have to admit, listening is a skill I had to learn. Talking is much more natural for me. My mother used to tell everyone, "At six months John started talking and he never stopped." It's true. I never run out of words to say. I like to set the tone. I like to entertain. I like to teach and mentor. But talking isn't learning. Listening is. Columnist Doug Larson said, "Wisdom is the reward you get for a lifetime of listening when you would have preferred to talk." I try to keep that in mind. If you're a talker, you should, too.

5. Teachable People Learn Something New Every Day

The secret to any person's success can be found in his or her daily agenda. People grow and improve, not by huge leaps and bounds but by small, incremental changes. A single day is enough to make us a little larger or a little smaller. Several single days strung together will make us a lot larger or a lot smaller. If you want to become a teachable person who learns from losses, then make learning your daily habit. It may not change your life in a day. But it will change your days for life.

Daily Practices to Become More Teachable

If you believe in the idea of trying to learn something new every day, but you don't know the best way to go about it, then I recommend that you do the following things every day.

1. Preparation

If you want to be ready to meet whatever challenges you're going to face on a given day and learn from them, you need to be prepared. That means working in advance—every day. As my old mentor John Wooden used to say, "When opportunity comes, it's too late to prepare."

As a student, you may feel like you're being challenged to learn all the time, whether you want to or not. But as I'm sure you've already figured out, learning doesn't just happen. There are things we all can do to prepare for it. Everything from completing your homework, to studying for a test, to organizing your bookbag. All of those things make you ready to learn the next time you're in school. You can prepare even more if you start each day with some specific questions:

- Where are my potential learning moments for today?
- Who will I meet and what can I learn from them?
- What will I experience and what might I be able to learn from it?

By looking for possible teaching moments and preparing for them, you make learning more likely.

2. Contemplation

As I mentioned in chapter 5 (on Improvement), time alone is essential to learning. Contemplation is taking time to observe and reflect on the things that happen in your life and find meaning in them. Allowing ourselves to stop and think gives us perspective on both the successes and failures of our day so that we can find the lessons within them. It also enables you to plan how you can improve in the future.

It's good to remember that there's a lot to learn from negative experiences. In science, mistakes always come before discoveries. It is impossible to make discoveries without making a bunch of errors first. To a scientist, a mistake is not failure—it's feedback. Using that feedback, a scientist can ask not just "What happened?" but also "What does it mean?"

JOURNAL IT!

Think about the past twenty-four hours. Have you discovered some new learning opportunities? Write in your journal the answers to the following questions and think about how you can apply what you've learned:

- What can I learn from what I read today?
- What can I learn from what I saw today?
- What can I learn from what I heard today?
- What can I learn from what I experienced today?
- What can I learn from what I did wrong today?
- What can I learn from whom I met today?
- What can I learn from what I discussed today?

I recommend that you set aside ten minutes every evening to think about that day, contemplating what happened and what you can learn from it. Not only will that help you to remain teachable, but you will also learn something every day because of the process.

3. Application

The true value of teachability comes when we take something that we learn and apply it. We can learn a lot from our mistakes if we remain teachable. Not everyone does that. When people make mistakes, they generally do one of three things in response to them: They resolve to never make another mistake, which is impossible. They allow their mistake to turn them into cowards, which is foolish. Or they make up their minds to learn from their mistake and apply the lesson to their lives, which helps them grow and become better.

Teachability Is for Everyone

It's easy to think that teachability is for certain types of people—maybe athletes or students. But in reality, we all need to be teachable. And teachability doesn't require perfect circumstances or an easy life. I believe teachability is an attitude, a mind-set that teachable people carry with them wherever they go and whatever they experience.

You become more teachable every time you focus more on the lesson to be learned than on how others see you. If you make it a higher priority to understand than to be understood, you'll take the most important steps toward learning.

8

Adversity: The Catalyst for Learning

In the Memphis, Tennessee, foster care system, Michael Oher was known as a "runner." From the time he was removed from his drug-addicted mother's custody and placed in a foster home, Michael wouldn't stay put. Instead, he repeatedly ran back to his mother's house. He writes in his book, *I Beat the Odds*, "I just wanted to get back to my mother, to try to pretend that the normal life I wanted so much was waiting for me there."[42] But from his earliest memory, Michael's life had never been normal.

His mother loved her twelve children, but "she seemed to love the crack pipe even more," Michael writes.[43] She often abandoned the kids—often for days at a time—to get high. She simply locked the door of the apartment and left. Locked out of their own home, the children fended for themselves, usually finding a neighbor who would feed them and let them spend the night. Even when their mom was home, life was never stable. She could never seem to keep an apartment and was regularly evicted, so they moved around a lot.

You may be familiar with some of Michael's story if you've seen the movie *The Blind Side*. It portrays Michael as a homeless teenager who is taken in by the Tuohy family, plays football for a private school, and becomes a star left tackle. He eventually ends up in the National Football League. The movie chronicles the last year of Michael's high school career, focusing mostly on the Tuohys' efforts to help him overcome his previous circumstances.

But as you might imagine, there's always more to the story. It turns out that Michael didn't succeed just because of the Tuohys' intervention; he had been working to overcome his circumstances for many years before they met.

There was always something different about Michael Oher. From age seven, he knew his path. "I watched the NBA finals between the Chicago Bulls and the Phoenix Suns," he writes, "and I knew—I knew—that sports were going to be my way out."[44] This was the era of the superstar Michael Jordan, and Oher watched in awe as Jordan helped his team win the championship. Oher himself was already big for his age, and athletic and fast. He'd played plenty of pickup basketball and football, and people seemed to think he should play organized sports. "I realized pretty early on," he said, "that I had a unique combination of build and talents."[45]

In contrast to how he was portrayed in the movie, Michael did know how to play football before he met the Tuohys. He had played a lot of basketball and football by then, in school and for a local league. And Michael didn't just play those sports—he studied them. He wanted to understand everything about them—from positions to overall strategy. He was determined to keep improving.

Surrounded by people who lived only for the day, Michael was focused on the future. As he got older and grew to understand that he wouldn't find a normal life with his mother, he began to look for a way out. But Michael didn't just rely on his sports prowess to succeed. He saw very early that the kids who had a chance of succeeding stayed away from certain behaviors like getting in trouble or doing drugs, and instead worked hard in school. He gravitated to those friends and did his best to succeed academically.

By the time he met the Tuohys, Michael had already done everything he could to change his circumstances. "I've never struggled with the question of whether I could succeed," he writes. "I only struggled with how. I was going to find a way, one way or another. I wasn't sure of the exact path, but I knew I wasn't going to give up until I'd achieved a better life for myself." He later adds, "And one family stepped up to the line to help me steer through it all."[46]

When he moved in with the Tuohys full-time for his senior year of high school, Michael knew where he needed to grow: in academics. With a grade point average of only 0.76, he needed to improve his grades in every subject. Having attended many schools growing up, with little encouragement to study, do homework, or even attend class, Michael needed to learn *how* to learn. The Tuohys hired a tutor for him, who worked with him for four hours a day. They later helped him take some online courses that could be used to replace the low grades he'd received early in his high school career.

In college at Ole Miss, Michael showed that he could learn. He earned high grades in all his courses, making the Chancellor's List more than once. He also scored nearly thirty points higher in an IQ test than what had been recorded for him in the public-school systems when he was growing up.[47]

Michael Oher has been playing in the NFL since 2009, and he continues to excel athletically. He works hard year-round, intent on pushing himself to reach his potential. He writes, "Making it to the pros wasn't the finish line for me. The world is full of people who got their big shot and then never did anything with it. I had come too far to just let being drafted be the end of my story."[48]

The *If* Factor

Writer and professor Robertson Davies said, "Extraordinary people survive under the most terrible circumstances and they become more extraordinary because of it." Michael's early circumstances were certainly challenging. But he succeeded in spite of them. The pain he experienced made him who he was and became the catalyst for change. He used adversity to make himself smarter—and better.

I believe that one of the times people change is when they hurt enough that they have to. Adversity causes pain and is a prompt for change. Most of the time we don't choose our adversity, but all the time we can choose our response to it. *If* we respond positively to difficulties, the outcome will be potentially positive. *If* we respond negatively to our difficulties, the outcome will be potentially negative. That's why I call our response "the *if* factor."

The Advantages of Adversity

Adversity is a catalyst for learning. It can actually create advantages for you *if* you face it with the right mind-set. It all depends on how you respond to it. Here's what I mean:

1. Adversity Introduces Us to Ourselves If *We Want It To*

Adversity always gets our attention. We can't ignore it. It causes us to stop and look at our situation. And at ourselves if we have the courage. Adversity is an opportunity for self-discovery. As the great Egyptian leader Anwar el-Sadat said, "Great suffering builds up a human being and puts him within the reach of self-knowledge." This I believe is true—if we embrace it that way.

Unfortunately, many people choose to hide during times of adversity. They withdraw from friends or family. They try to distract themselves. They do whatever they can to avoid dealing with the reality of the situation.

One of my favorite books is *As a Man Thinketh* by James Allen. My father made me read it when I was in my early teens. One of the ideas that left the strongest impression on me then was this: "Circumstance does not make the man; it reveals him to himself." That is true, but only *if* you allow it to.

Adversity has introduced me to myself many times during my lifetime. It has opened my eyes. It has gone deep into of my heart. It has tested my strength. And it has taught me a lot. Here are a few of the lessons I've learned:

- When I have gotten off track and am seemingly lost, I have learned that the road to success is not always a clear, straight road.
- When I have been exhausted and frustrated, I have learned that trying times are not the time to stop trying.
- When I have been discouraged with my progress, I have learned not to let what I was doing get to me before I got to it.
- When I have failed, I have learned that I will not be judged by the number of times I fail but by the number of times I succeed.

2. Adversity Is a Better Teacher Than Success If *We Let It Teach Us*

Adversity comes to us as a teaching tool. You've probably heard the saying, "When the student is ready, the teacher will come." That is not necessarily true. With adversity, the teacher will come whether the student is ready or not. Those who are ready learn from the teacher. Those who are not don't learn.

Philosopher and author Emmet Fox said, "It is the Law that any difficulties that can come to you at any time, no matter what they are, must be exactly what you need most at the moment, to enable you to take the next step forward by overcoming them. The only real misfortune, the only real tragedy, comes when we suffer without learning the lesson." The key to avoiding that tragedy is *wanting* to learn from life's difficulties.

Oprah Winfrey's advice to "turn your wounds into wisdom" can come true for us only *if* we want to learn from our wounds. It requires the right mind-set and a deliberate intention to find the lesson in the loss. If we don't embrace those things, then all we end up with is the scars.

JOURNAL IT!

In your journal, make two lists: the best things that have ever happened to you, and the worst things. For each item, write one thing you learned. If you're like most people, your more valuable lessons came from the hardship list. Adversity is hard, but it can yield great rewards if we use the lessons that it gives to learn and grow.

3. Adversity Opens Doors for New Opportunities If *We Want to Take Them*

One of the greatest lessons I've learned as a leader is that adversity is often the door to opportunity. Michael Oher was shaped by his early hard experiences. They certainly had negative effects. But his drive and determination also grew in that environment. And then because he looked for opportunities all the time, he was able to overcome his circumstances and excel in many areas.

When you face adversity, it's easy to let it get you down. After all, it's often painful and hard. But adversity can reveal opportunities if we're willing to look for it. Inventor Alexander Graham Bell, who invented the telephone, said, "When one door closes, another opens; but we often look so long and so regretfully upon the closed door that we do not see the one which has opened for us." Don't let yourself focus so much on the adversity that you miss an opportunity.

4. Adversity Brings Good Things If *We Expect It and Plan for It*

In life we should all expect pain. It's a part of life. It's a part of loss. The question is, are you going to let it stop you from doing what you want and need to do?

In the movie *Black Hawk Down* a vehicle filled with wounded American soldiers lurches to a stop in the middle of a street where Somali bullets are flying in every direction. The officer in charge tells a soldier to get in and start driving.

"I can't," says the soldier. "I'm shot."

"We're all shot," responds the officer. "Get in and drive!"

In everyday life, if you're going to endure the pain it takes to compete, why not compete to win? No one ever says, "Go for the silver." Athletes, coaches, and fans always say, "Go for the gold!" Why? Because gold represents the best.

Successful people expect to experience pain when they face adversity. They plan for it. And by planning for it, they set themselves up to benefit from it. Fred Smith once said, "I listened to Bob Richards, the Olympic gold medalist, interview younger Olympic winners of the gold. He asked them, 'What did you do when you began to hurt?'" Fred points out that none of the Olympians were surprised by the question. They expected pain, and they had a strategy for dealing with it. As Bob Richards summed up, "You never win the gold without hurting."

5. Adversity Writes Our Story and If Our Response Is Right, the Story Will Be a Good One

Some people treat adversity as a stepping-stone, others as a tombstone. The difference in the way they approach it depends on how they see it. Performance psychologist Jim Loehr says, "Champions have taught us how to take an experience and essentially write the story of its effect. If you see a failure as an opportunity to learn and get better, it will be. If you perceive it as a mortal blow, it will be. In that way, the power of the story is more important than the experience itself."

Adversity without triumph is not inspiring; it's depressing. Adversity without growth is not encouraging; it's discouraging. The great potential story in adversity is one of hope and success. Adversity is everyone's, but the story you write with your life is yours alone. Everyone gets a chance to be the hero in a potentially great story. Some step up to that role and some don't. The choice is yours.

JOURNAL IT!

What kind of movie would portray the adversity in your life? Like Michael Oher, we all have the opportunity to rewrite our story, to use adversity to achieve something amazing. Think of your story so far, with all the adversity you've faced. What kind of triumphal ending would you like to see? Write down that new ending.

9

Problems: Opportunities for Learning

Have you heard of the movie *Frozen*? The 2014 film was so popular that you probably know the plot even if you haven't seen it. You might even have its hit song, "Let It Go," memorized, whether you wanted to or not. On the Disney soundtrack, this song about overcoming adversity is sung by actress and singer Demi Lovato.

Demi's life has had its share of problems. She's been open with her fans about her struggles with bullying, self-image, addiction, eating issues, and cutting. But she didn't get to record the single in spite of her issues, but because of them. "It just so happened that Demi was part of the Disney family already, and that she had a past that she's pretty open about that is similar to Elsa's journey of leaving a dark past and fear behind and moving forward with your power," says songwriter Kristen Anderson-Lopez.[49]

Demi Lovato responded to her problems by getting help, seeking professional treatment in 2010. Since then, she's continued to live life in the spotlight, sharing honestly about her journey toward health. She's guest-starred on the TV show *Glee* and had a regular spot on *The X-Factor*. And her album from 2013 had several hit singles.

From Demi's perspective, "Let It Go" was a perfect fit. In a statement, she said, "It's so relatable. Elsa is finding her identity; she's growing into who she is and she's finally accepting her own strength and magical powers. Instead of hiding it, like she's done all her life, she's letting it go and embracing it."[50]

Whenever I feel like problems are going to overwhelm me, and I'm in danger of getting discouraged, I try to remind myself that I'm not alone in my experience. You may have seen the popular quote by an unknown author: "Everyone has problems. Some people are just better at hiding them than others." If you spend a lot of time on social media, you may be led to believe that you're the only one who has problems... that everyone else has it all together. But what's shared on Facebook is often not the whole picture.

The reality is that problems exist for everyone. We all have battles to fight and issues to resolve. We can't control whether we're going to have problems, but we can control how we respond to them.

Don't Do This...

The key to overcoming problems and learning from them is to approach them the right way. Over the years, I've learned that problems get better or worse based on what you do or don't do when you face them. First, let me give you the don'ts:

1. Don't Underestimate the Problem

Many problems go unresolved or are managed ineffectively because we do not take them seriously enough. Years ago I read a wonderful book by Robert H. Schuller entitled *Tough Times Never Last, But Tough People Do!* The following paragraph helped me as a young leader to find a more realistic view of my problems and myself:

> Never underestimate a problem or your power to cope with it. Realize that the problem you are facing has been faced by millions of human beings. You have untapped potential for dealing with a problem if you will take the problem and your own undeveloped, unchanneled powers seriously. Your reaction to a problem, as much as the problem itself, will determine the outcome.
>
> I have seen people face the most catastrophic problems with a positive mental attitude, turning their problems into creative experiences. They turned their scars into stars.[51]

When I first read that paragraph, I became inspired. It made me believe that the size of the person is more important than the size of the problem.

Our perspective on problems is so important. Shug Jordan, a former football and basketball coach at Auburn University, was reported to be explaining to one of his new coaches how to recruit ball players for the team when he asked, "Do we want the player who gets knocked down but doesn't get back up?"

"No," said the new coach, "we don't want him."

"Do we want the player who gets knocked down, gets back up, gets knocked down, gets back up, gets knocked down, gets back up?"

"Yes," said the new coach, "we want him!"

"No, we don't," said Jordan. "We want the guy who keeps knocking everyone down!" The bigger the person, the smaller the problem.

2. Don't Overestimate the Problem

Some people experience one problem three or more times. They experience it the first time when they worry about the problem. They experience it the second time when it actually occurs. And they experience it again as they keep reliving it! I've done that. Have you? When faced with a problem, my first instinct is often to exaggerate its impact. Do that and you may be defeated before the problem ever occurs!

Cy Young was one of the greatest pitchers in major league baseball. After his career was over, he commented on the tendencies of managers to take their starters out of the game at the slightest hint of trouble. He observed, "In our day when a pitcher got into trouble in a game, instead of taking him out, our manager would leave him in and tell him to pitch his way out of trouble." Sometimes the problem is not as big of a problem as we anticipate, and by tackling it, we shrink it down in size.

3. Don't Wait for the Problem to Solve Itself

That brings us to the next lesson I've learned about problems. You can't wait for them to solve themselves. Patience is a virtue in problem solving if you are at the same time doing all that you can to fix the situation. It is not a virtue if you are waiting, hoping that the problem will solve itself or just go away.

Problems demand that we pay them attention. Why? Because left alone they almost always get worse.

JOURNAL IT!

What problem are you currently facing that you've been hoping would solve itself? You need to recognize that that's unlikely, and come up with a course of action for solving it. Turn to your journal and write down specific steps you can take to move the problem toward a solution. Do step one today or tomorrow at the latest.

4. Don't Make the Problem Worse

Not only do problems not solve themselves, but we can actually make them worse by how we respond to them. For years I've told people that problems are like fires, and every person carries around two buckets. One bucket has water, and the other gasoline. When you come across a problem, you can use the bucket of water to try to put the fire out. Or you can pour gasoline on it and make it explode. Same problem, two different results.

Taking a potentially explosive situation and making it worse is only one way of aggravating a problem. We can also make problems worse when we respond to them poorly. Some of the ways we can do that include:

- Losing our perspective
- Giving up important priorities and values
- Losing our sense of humor
- Feeling sorry for ourselves
- Blaming others for our situation

Instead, we need to try to remain positive and take action to solve the problem. Author Norman Vincent Peale asserted, "Positive thinking is how you think about a problem. Enthusiasm is how you feel about a problem. The two together determine what you do about a problem."

Do This...

If you want to overcome problems and turn them into opportunities for learning, then I recommend that you do the following:

1. Do Anticipate the Problem

They say the punch that knocks you out is not necessarily the hardest one, but the one you didn't see coming. I once read about a prisoner in Sydney, Australia, who succeeded in breaking out of jail. He hid on the underside of a delivery truck that had stopped briefly in the prison warehouse. He held on desperately as the truck drove out of the prison. A few moments later, when the truck finally stopped, the prisoner dropped down to the ground and rolled outward to freedom. Unfortunately, he discovered that he was now in the courtyard of another prison five miles from the first. He sure didn't see that coming.

Of course, anticipating problems doesn't mean worrying all the time about everything that *could* go wrong. You need to find a balance between thinking ahead and becoming a worrywart. Be aware of what could happen, without focusing all of your attention on it.

2. Do Communicate the Problem

Problems happen to everyone, and tackling them often involves other people. Whether the other person is affected by the problem, can help solve the problem, or *is* the problem, it's important to communicate about what's going wrong. Lack of communication and poor communication not only prevent us from solving problems; they can also create problems of their own.

If you're having a problem with one person specifically, try to talk to him or her about the issue. By learning their point of view, you may realize that there isn't really a problem at all, just a miscommunication. Or you may figure out a solution that neither of you had thought about before. Talking to family, friends, teachers, and teammates will help you to solve problems big and small.

Do you have a problem that you haven't yet told anyone about? You already know that problems don't solve themselves. The first step is often to talk about it. Find someone who cares about you and tell them what's going on. Remember, though, your goal in sharing the problem is to grow and change, not just complain. Ask for this person's feedback and allow their outside perspective to help you view the problem differently.

3. Do Evaluate the Problem

They say you should never open a can of worms unless you plan to go fishing. Too often, I've been quick to open up the can without first thinking through the situation. I would have been better off trying to evaluate first.

How do you do that? First, you need to ask yourself, *How important is the issue at hand?* If someone wrongly asserts that the moon is a hundred miles from Earth, no big deal. Let it go. Unless you're in science class, it doesn't matter. It's not a problem you need to deal with. If someone is about to eat food that is poisoned, deal with it immediately. You have to determine the size and weight of each problem individually. Sometimes that's hard to do, especially for a person who wants to jump in on every little thing. To keep myself from doing that, for years I had a laminated card on my desk that asked, "Does this REALLY MATTER?" It helped me keep perspective when an issue was being discussed.

The second question you need to ask is, *Who is involved?* Often problems are problems because of the people in the middle of them. Some are like Charlie Brown in the classic *Peanuts* television special, *A Charlie Brown Christmas*. When he just can't seem to get into the Christmas spirit, Linus tells him, "You're the only person I know who can take a wonderful season like Christmas and turn it into a problem." Knowing who is involved allows you to target the solution toward the specific person and his or her personality.

As you evaluate problems, try to keep a realistic perspective, and always keep the end goal in mind.

4. Do Appreciate the Problem

Appreciating a problem is the opposite of what most of us want to do! Most people see a problem as a negative and try to avoid it. However, if we have the right attitude and appreciate a problem for how it can help us grow, not only will we work harder to solve it, but we will also learn and grow from it. Problems always bring opportunities, and opportunities often bring new problems. The two go hand in hand. If we can learn to appreciate that truth, we have a real advantage in life.

The way an eagle uses the challenge of turbulent winds is a fantastic illustration of the benefits a problem can have.

- *Turbulent winds cause the eagle to fly higher.* There is tremendous lifting power in the thermal updrafts of turbulent winds. These updrafts cause the eagle to reach great heights as he soars with them.
- *Turbulent winds give the eagle a larger view.* The higher the eagle flies, the larger his perspective of the land below him will be. From this higher position the sharp eyes of the eagle are able to see much more.
- *Turbulent winds lift the eagle above harassment.* At lower elevations the eagle is often bothered by suspicious crows, disgruntled hawks, and other smaller

birds. As the eagle soars higher, he leaves behind all these distractions.

- *Turbulent winds allow the eagle to use less effort.* The wings of the eagle are designed for gliding in the winds. The feather structure prevents stalling, reduces the turbulence, and produces a relatively smooth ride with minimum effort—even in rough winds.

- *Turbulent winds allow the eagle to stay up longer.* The eagle uses winds to soar and glide for long periods of time. In the winds, the eagle first glides in long shallow circles downward and then spirals upward with a thermal updraft.

- *Turbulent winds help the eagle to fly faster.* Normally, the eagle flies at a speed of about fifty miles an hour. However, when he glides in wind currents, speeds of well over one hundred miles per hour are not uncommon.[52]

A problem isn't really a problem unless you allow it to be one. A problem is really an opportunity to learn something new. If you can see it that way, then every time you face a problem, you will realize that you're actually faced with an opportunity. At the least, it's an opportunity to learn. But it could become a path to success if you pursue solving it with the right attitude.

10

Bad Experiences:
The Perspective for Learning

The last thing then-fifteen-year-old Malala Yousafzai remembers is being on the bus on her way home from school. The next thing she knew, she was waking in a hospital in Birmingham, England. It was a week later.

That was back in October 2012. She later learned how it happened. A young man had flagged down the school bus in their small town in Pakistan, then jumped in the back where all the schoolgirls were and asked, "Who is Malala?" No one spoke, but the girls looked at Malala, accidentally revealing her identity. The gunman then shot her in the head at point-blank range. But the bullet miraculously missed her brain, and Malala survived the assassination attempt on her life.

In the hospital, without being told, she believed she knew what had happened to her. "Was I shot?" she asked Dr. Fiona Reynolds. After the doctor described what had happened, Malala said to herself, "So they did it."[53] Malala wasn't surprised, because she had been threatened by the Taliban for years—ever since she'd started blogging and speaking out about their violent opposition to girls' education in her home country of Pakistan.

She was already fairly well known for her blog and appearances in documentaries, but something happened while Malala was in the hospital. Suddenly the world was completely focused on her and her cause. The press flocked to Birmingham and reported on every little change in her status as she recovered.

The bad experience was having a positive outcome. Malala became a symbol for the importance of education for children worldwide. As the UN's special envoy on global education, Gordon Brown, later said, "Because of Malala, there is a public understanding that something is wrong and has got to be done."[54]

Many people in her position might have hidden or given up. Not Malala. In July 2013, after making a full recovery, Malala Yousafzai spoke before a special youth assembly at the United Nations headquarters in New York. "They thought that the bullets would silence us, but they failed," she said. "And then, out of that silence, came thousands of voices." She called for a global commitment to education for all children, saying, "One child, one teacher, one book, one pen can change the world."[55]

The horrible actions of the Taliban had turned into an opportunity for Malala and her supporters. And she has used that opportunity to influence many lives. In late 2013, her book, *I Am Malala*, came out. In 2014, she received the Nobel Peace Prize. And she also founded the Malala Fund,[56] dedicated to providing educational opportunities for girls who have been denied a formal education because of social, economic, legal, or political factors. They do so by working within local communities, seeking creative solutions that empower girls to live up to their potential.

Malala continues to live with her family and go to school in England, but she hopes that they will eventually be able to return to Pakistan. She continues to speak up for those who are denied an education. And the world continues to listen. As Mishal Husain wrote for the BBC, "When I ask her what she thinks the militants achieved that day, she smiles. 'I think they may be regretting that they shot Malala,' she says. 'Now she is heard in every corner of the world.' "[57]

Putting Your Losses into Perspective

Obviously, no one goes out of the way to have bad experiences. Sometimes we do stupid things and have to live with unexpected consequences. Others times we are victims of bad experiences, as Malala was. But the truth is that the negative experiences we have can do us some good, if we are willing to let them. That can be true even of the worst of them.

The next time you have a bad experience, allow it to help you do the following:

1. Accept Your Humanness

No matter how hard we try, no matter how talented we are, no matter how high our standards may be, we will fail sometimes. And we will be hurt by other people. Why? Because we're all human. Nobody is perfect, and when we have bad experiences, we should allow that to be a reminder to us that we need to accept our imperfections.

When you have a bad experience, I hope you will give yourself some leeway—whether it's a matter beyond your control or because you make a mistake. You're only human, and you shouldn't expect yourself to be perfect.

Q&A WITH JOHN

Q: Isn't this a book about growth? Doesn't accepting your humanness mean you need to accept yourself as you are and not try to change?

A: It's important to find balance. Accepting your humanness means understanding that you can't be perfect, so you shouldn't beat yourself up for your failures. When you accept and admit your mistakes, you can be free to focus on growing and improving.

2. Learn to Laugh at Yourself and Life

I have discovered that if I'm willing see the humor in my bad experiences, I will never run out of things to laugh about. Does laughing fix everything? Maybe not. But it helps.

Sometimes it's hard to see the humor during a difficult experience. Often I say to myself, "This is not funny today, but tomorrow it may be." How much lighter would your load be if you were to find ways to laugh when you were faced with bad experiences?

3. Keep the Right Perspective

Author and speaker Denis Waitley says, "Mistakes are painful when they happen, but years later a collection of mistakes is what is called experience." Seeing difficulties as experience is a matter of perspective. It's like the difference between going in the ocean as a small child and as a young adult. When you're little, the waves look massive and you fear that they may overwhelm you. When you're older, the same size waves may be seen as a source of fun or relaxation.

When facing difficulties, maintaining perspective isn't always easy, but it is worth fighting for. As you work to maintain the right point of view, try to keep these three things in mind:

> *When you have a bad experience, which one of the following phrases is most likely to represent your thinking?*
>
> *a. I never wanted to do that task to start with, so who cares?*
> *b. I'm a failure and my life is over.*
> *c. I want to give up and never try again.*
> *d. I'm gaining experience from my mistakes; I wonder if I can get some help.*
> *e. I now know three ways that won't work, so I'll try again.*
>
> *Your answer says more about your perspective than it does about the bad experience. That's why the responses to the same bad experience can be so varied. Make a commitment to try to respond with answers like d or e in the future.*

Don't Base Your Self-Worth on a Bad Experience

You are not your performance or your grades. And you don't have to be defined by your worst moments. So don't base your self-image on a bad game, a failed quiz, or a botched speech in front of your class. Instead, try to understand and accept your value as a human being. If you fail, don't ever tell yourself, "I am a failure." Instead, keep things in perspective and say, "I may have messed up that audition, but I'm still okay. I can still be a winner!"

Don't Feel Sorry for Yourself

One of the worst ways to lose perspective is to start feeling sorry for yourself. Okay, if you have a bad experience, you can feel sorry for yourself for twenty-four hours, but after that, pick yourself up and get moving again. Because if you start to wallow, you just might get stuck.

Psychiatrist Frederic Flach, in his book *Resilience*, points out that survivors of bad experiences don't let the negatives in their lives define them, and they don't wallow in self-pity. They don't believe their negative experience is the worst thing in the world. Instead, they think, *What happened to me may have been bad, but other people are worse off. I'm not giving in.*

If you find yourself in the aftermath of a bad experience, try to focus on the good you can make of the difficulty. Because of the experience you've gained, you may even be able to help others who have gone through similar difficulties.

Do Consider Your Failures as a Process
to Learn and Improve

When we fail or have a bad experience, we need to learn to become more like scientists and inventors. When their work fails, they call it an experiment that didn't work. Or they say they tested a hypothesis. Or they term it data collection. They keep this perspective, avoid taking it personally, learn from it, and use it for future success. What a great way to look at things.

4. Don't Give Up

Swimmer Eric Shanteau has called the 2004 U.S. Olympic Swim Trials "the most devastating experience of my life." That's quite a statement considering Shanteau was diagnosed with cancer in 2008. What would make those Olympic trials such a difficult experience? He finished third—and only the first two places in the trials make the Olympic team. In fact, it happened twice during those trials. He missed second place in the 400-meter individual medley by 0.99 seconds and the 200-meter individual medley by 0.34 seconds. Shanteau recalls,

> The initial reaction was anger. I remember walking down that deck being very frustrated. You see a lifelong goal slip out of your fingers in the last five meters and it's brutal. It was very, very hard. I didn't

want anything to do with the sport for about seven weeks after. Finishing third at the trials, you might as well get last.[58]

He may have wanted to give up, but he didn't. He got back in the pool and trained for another four years. His reward in 2008 was making the team in the 200-meter breaststroke. Though he didn't medal in Beijing, he did swim a personal best. He kept training and returned to the Olympics again in 2012 in London. He won a gold medal by swimming the breaststroke for the team in the 4×100-meter medley relay.

What does Shanteau know about bad experiences that most people don't? He knows that:

- When it comes to setbacks, there are two kinds of people: splatters, who hit rock bottom, fall apart, and stay on the bottom; and bouncers, who hit the bottom, pull themselves together, and bounce back up.
- Failure is the cost of seeking new challenges.
- Success lies in having made the effort; failure lies in never having tried.
- Most failures are people who have the habit of making excuses.
- Ninety percent of those who fail are not actually defeated; they simply quit.

If you want to succeed in life, you can't give up.

5. Don't Let Your Bad Experiences Become Worse Experiences

One thing that's worse than a bad experience is letting that bad experience become an even worse one—if you have the power to stop it. How do you gain the power to recognize when an experience is going from bad to worse? By learning from previous experiences using critical thinking skills.

If you find yourself in a bad experience, one of the first things you should try to do is determine if the bad experience is a result of ignorance or stupidity. Ignorance means that you didn't have the necessary knowledge to do the right thing. A person can hardly be blamed for that. Stupidity is the result of knowing what to do but not using that knowledge in your actions.

BAD EXPERIENCES BASED ON IGNORANCE	BAD EXPERIENCES BASED ON STUPIDITY
"I didn't know better, so I did it."	"I knew better, but I did it anyway."
"I didn't know better, so I didn't do it."	"I knew better, yet I didn't do it."

Bad experiences based on ignorance require learning. If you have a teachable spirit, as I discussed in chapter 7, not only can you stop a bad experience from getting worse, you can make it better. On the other hand, bad experiences based on stupidity usually come from lack of discipline and poor choices. Changing those requires a change in behavior. If you don't make those changes, the bad experiences will likely keep coming and keep getting worse.

6. Let the Bad Experience Lead You to a Good Experience

Everyone can relate to having bad experiences in life. But not everyone works to turn the bad experiences into good ones. That is possible only when we turn our losses into learning experiences. You just have to remember that bad experiences are bad only if we fail to learn from them. And good experiences are almost always a result of previous bad experiences.

His Bad Experience Was His Springboard

As you face bad experiences, it's important for you to remember that you can rarely see the good while you're stuck in the bad. You usually gain perspective on the other side of it. That was certainly the case for Giuseppe, who was named for his father, an immigrant from Italy who had settled in

California. Because they lived in America, the family called him Joe. But his father had his own nickname for him: Good-for-Nothing. Why did the elder Giuseppe call him that? Because Joe hated fishing. That was seen as a terrible thing by the father, because he was a fisherman. He loved the fishing business. So did all of his sons—except for Good-for-Nothing Joe. The boy didn't like being on the boat, and the smell of fish made him sick. It was a bad experience for young Joe, all around.

The boy offered to work in the office or to repair nets, but his father was simply disgusted with him and said he was good for nothing.

The boy, who was not afraid of hard work, delivered newspapers and shined shoes, giving the money to the family, but since it wasn't fishing, the elder Giuseppe saw no value in it.

Young Joe hated fishing, but he loved baseball. His older brother used to play sandlot ball, and Joe used to follow him there. And he was good—something of a legend among his playmates. When Joe was sixteen, he decided to drop out of school to become a baseball player. By the time he was through with baseball, he was a legend. He was christened as Giuseppe, but the nation came to know him as Joe DiMaggio, called the most complete player of his generation.

And his father, the elder Giuseppe, what did he think about it? Though he had wanted all of his sons to enter the family business, he was finally proud of his son and respected his accomplishments. How could he not? Joe had experienced his father's rejection, but didn't let it stop him from pursuing success. He found it in baseball, turning a bad experience into a great experience through the perspective of learning.

11

Change: The Price of Learning

It's pretty hard to imagine a world without smartphones today. With more than 70 percent of Americans using them as of 2014,[59] they're an ordinary part of everyday life. But as recently as 2006, the smartphone that we take for granted didn't exist. The idea of one device that could make a phone call, text, surf the Internet, send an e-mail, play music, show videos, and provide games was crazy.

But for one man, no new idea was crazy. Steve Jobs of Apple thrived on "new" and embraced change. "I think if you do something and it turns out pretty good," he said, "then you should go do something else wonderful, not dwell on it for too long. Just figure out what's next."[60]

Jobs had been back at Apple only since 1996, after an eleven-year absence from the company he'd founded in 1976. While he was away, he'd revolutionized movie animation with the purchase and development of Pixar Animation Studios.

When he came back to Apple, he quickly made changes and streamlined the company, which had actually been dying. And he oversaw the big turnaround for Apple in 2001, with the introduction of the iPod, a simple but elegant MP3 player.

Very soon, people began asking for a phone in the iPod, so they could carry just one device. But Steve Jobs just wasn't interested at first. Apple had never been in the phone business. And the technology didn't exist in a small enough size.

Some people would have dismissed the idea and moved on. But Steve Jobs was open to change.

"He had the ability to change his mind, much more so than anyone I've ever met," says Tim Cook, Apple's current CEO, about Jobs. "Maybe the most underappreciated thing about Steve was that he had the courage to change his mind."[61]

Soon Steve Jobs began to get a vision for what an Apple phone could and should be able to do. It was probably more than anyone else had ever imagined. He wanted it to have a touchscreen that could be used without a stylus. It would have an onscreen keyboard rather than a physical one like that on a BlackBerry. He wanted users to be able to switch from one task to another, like making a call, then searching for a map and texting directions to a friend. Jobs pushed his designers and engineers to create an iPhone that could do all that and more. It took more than two years, but in the end the iPhone was created, and it was a huge success. What may seem normal and ordinary to you was as revolutionary as the car or electricity. The iPhone became the prototype for all the smartphones that came after it.

Soon after the iPhone was released, smartphones exploded. Almost every year, Apple introduced a new version of the iPhone. Google introduced Android phones late in 2007, and their operating system has grown to be more popular than Apple's iOS. Now smartphones are made by half a dozen manufacturers, and nearly everyone has one.

The smartphone as we know it was created because Steve Jobs thrived on change. In an interview in 1994, he described his philosophy this way:

> When you grow up, you tend to get told that the world is the way it is and your [goal] is just to live your life inside the world, try not to bash into the walls too much, try to have a nice family, have fun, save a little money. That's a very limited life. Life can be much broader, once you discover one simple fact, and that is that everything around you that you call life was made up by people that were no smarter than you. And you can change it, you can influence it, you can build your own things that other people can use. Once you learn that, you'll never be the same again.

The minute that you understand that you can poke life and actually something will, you know if you push in, something will pop out the other side, that you can change it, you can mold it. That's maybe the most important thing. It's to shake off this erroneous notion that life is there and you're just gonna live in it, versus embrace it, change it, improve it, make your mark upon it.

I think that's very important and however you learn that, once you learn it, you'll want to change life and make it better, 'cause it's kind of messed up, in a lot of ways. Once you learn that, you'll never be the same again.[62]

When Steve Jobs died of pancreatic cancer in 2011 at fifty-six years old, his creation of the smartphone had changed the way we live. Fred Vogelstein said it this way: "Ponder the individual impacts of the book, the newspaper, the telephone, the radio, the tape recorder, the camera, the video camera, the compass, the television, the VCR and the DVD, the personal computer, the cellphone, the video game and the iPod. The smartphone is all those things, and it fits in your pocket."[63]

Why People Resist Change

Steve Jobs said that people didn't recognize that they could create change. I would even take that one step further. They often *reject* change. Why is change not embraced by most people? Because...

Change Can Feel Like a Personal Loss

Novelist Andre Gide observed, "One doesn't discover new lands without consenting to lose sight of the shore for a very long time." You're probably looking forward to some big changes in coming years, whether you end up going off to college or moving out of your parents' house. When you do make those changes, you'll lose sight of one shore before reaching the next. That loss can be very frightening, and it can sometimes feel like a personal loss. But the truth of the matter is that though change *feels* personal, it isn't. The world keeps changing and it affects everyone, whether they like it or not.

Poet and philosopher Ralph Waldo Emerson said, "We lose something for everything we gain." We like gaining, but we don't like losing. We want to have the one without the other. But life doesn't work that way. As the ancient Roman philosopher Seneca said, "Every new beginning comes from some other beginning's end." We are continually making trades in life. Unfortunately, if you resist change, you are trading your potential to grow for your comfort. No change means no growth.

Change Feels Awkward

Change always feels different. Because it's unfamiliar, it often doesn't feel right. Let me give you an example. Take a moment right now and clasp your hands together with your fingers interlaced. That probably feels very comfortable. Why? Because you naturally place your hands a certain way, with one thumb over the other. Now clasp your hands the opposite way by trading the position of your thumbs and moving your fingers over just one finger. How does that feel? It's probably uncomfortable. You never clasp your hands that way.

Is it wrong to clasp your hands this other way? No. Is it an inferior way of clasping hands? No. It's just different. And different feels awkward. But you *can* get used to it. Don't believe me? Every day for the next two weeks, clasp your hands the opposite way from what you're used to. By the end of that time, it will feel almost as comfortable as your natural way.

> As a young adult, you're in a season of tremendous change. Maybe that's why so much of life feels so awkward! You have a unique opportunity at your age to learn how to react

(Continued)

> *appropriately to the awkwardness of change, and make it a part of your life. Can you think of a new experience that felt awkward at the time but now seems pretty normal? Examples might include the first day of middle school or the first time you met your current best friend. Remember that awkwardness does eventually go away, and you'll be able to handle the changes that you need to experience in the future.*

Change Goes against Tradition

When I received my first leadership position in an organization, I can't tell you how many times I heard the phrase "We've never done it that way before." It seemed as if every time I wanted to make an improvement, I heard someone tell me why we should avoid making the change. It was frustrating, especially when the person who said it couldn't tell me *why* it had always been done the way it had been done.

Some people believe that nothing should ever be done until everyone is convinced that it ought to be done. The problem with that is it takes so long to convince them that by the time they finally agree to the change, it's time to move on to something else.

How People Respond to Change

Because people don't like change, most of them don't react to it very well. And their response creates more problems for them. Here's what I mean:

Most People Change Only Enough to Get Away from Problems, Not Enough to Fix Them

Most people would rather change things around them to improve their lives. But sometimes the root of a problem lies within yourself, and you have to take the time to make a change within yourself to make your life better. Working just hard enough to fix the problem without going after the root means that your problems will just keep coming back at you. If you want to get better, you need to be willing to change.

Most People Do the Same Thing the Same Way, Yet Expect Different Results

Whenever we try something and it fails, why do we keep trying the exact same thing expecting to get different results? It doesn't make sense. What do we expect to change? Our luck? The laws of physics? How can our lives get better if we don't change?

Our lives are like a trip we plan to a distant city. We set a destination, map out our route, and start driving. But we should know there will be detours and obstacles ahead. Do we ignore those and pretend they don't exist? How successful will we be if we think, *The obstacles and conditions need to adjust to me, because I'm not changing*? Not very. We need to be willing to make adjustments.

Most People See Change as a Hurtful Necessity Instead of a Helpful Opportunity

Let's face the fact: change is messy. But life is change. Being born was painful. Learning to eat was messy. Learning to walk was difficult *and* painful. In fact, most of the things you needed to learn in order to live were tough on you. But you didn't know any better, and you did what you needed to do to learn and grow. Now that you're older, you have a choice. Do you want to avoid the potential pain or endure it and pursue the opportunity? Every time you embrace change, there is an opportunity for you to go in a positive direction, make improvements to yourself, abandon old negative habits and ways of thinking. Change allows you to learn how you think, come up with new strategies, and build your relationships. Without change there is no innovation, creativity, or improvement. If you are open to change, you will have a better opportunity to manage it when it comes.

Most People Won't Pay the Immediate Price to Change and End Up Paying the Ultimate Price for Not Changing

My dad often said to me when I was faced with a decision that required discipline, "John, pay now so you can play later." That lesson was a constant theme in my life when I was growing up. Why? Because I always wanted to play! It was in my nature. But Dad kept telling me, "You can play now and pay later, or you can pay now and play later. But make no mistake: you will pay. And the longer you wait, the more you will pay, because delayed payment demands interest."

Change always requires something of us. We must pay a price for it. In fact, ongoing change and improvement require continual payment. But the process begins with the *first* payment. That first payment starts the growth process. If that first price remains unpaid, there is no growth or learning. And what will that cost you in the end? You lose potential and gain regret.

Most People Change Only When Prompted by One of Three Things

In the end, because people are so resistant to it, change occurs only under certain conditions. In my experience, people change when:

- They hurt enough that they have to
- They learn enough that they want to
- They receive enough that they are able to

Unless one of those things happens, people don't change. Sometimes people require all three to happen before they are willing to change. But you need to be willing to change before it gets to this point.

Making the Changes That Count

If you want to maximize your ability to pay the price of learning and set yourself up to change, improve, and grow, then you need to do the five following things:

1. Change Yourself

I noticed a long time ago that when people are not getting along, what each person wants most of all is for the other person to change. I believe that is part of being human: to look for the faults in others and ignore our own. But that's not how you improve any relationship.

My friend Tony Evans writes,

If you want a better world,
Composed of better nations,

Inhabited by better states,
Filled with better counties,
Made up of better cities,
Comprised of better neighborhoods,
Illuminated by better churches,
Populated by better families,
Then you'll have to start by becoming
A better person.

If you want to see positive change in your friendships, quit looking for better friends and become a better person. If you want to see positive change in your schoolwork, quit complaining about your teacher and become a better student. In life, if you want more, you must become more.

2. Change Your Attitude

Trying to change others is an exercise in futility. No one can change another person. I didn't always know this. For many years my life was filled with disappointments over other people's unwillingness to grow. But anything you try to change that is outside of your control will ultimately disappoint you. What's worse, when you try to change those things that are outside of your control, you can start to lose control of those things inside your control, because your focus is wrong. That's a trap to be avoided.

139

What's the solution? Changing your attitude. That is completely within your control, and this one change can be a major factor in changing your life for the positive. By choosing to think positively, you can minimize the negative effects of those around you who have bad attitudes. You can stop taking it personally when someone in your life won't change. You can see opportunities where once you saw obstacles. And as author and speaker Wayne Dyer says, "When you change the way you look at things, the things you look at actually begin to change."

3. Change Your Nongrowing Friends

There's an old saying: "A mirror reflects a man's face, but what he is really like is shown by the kind of friends he chooses." If you want to be a growing person, you need to spend time with growing people. If you want to be someone who embraces positive change, you need to hang around with positive learners.

Your friends will either help you stretch or choke your dreams. Some will inspire you to be better. Others will want you to join them on the couch of life where they do their least. Because not everyone wants to see you succeed, you have to make a choice. Are you going to let the people who aren't growing bring you down? Or are you going to move on? This can be a painful and difficult choice, but it can change your life for the better.

> *What is the impact of spending time with the wrong people? Ask yourself these questions:*
>
> - *What kind of advice do you receive when you seek it from unproductive people?*
> - *What happens when you discuss your problems with someone who doesn't care about solving them?*
> - *What happens when you follow someone who isn't going anywhere?*
> - *Where do you end up when you ask directions from someone who is lost?*
>
> *The fact of the matter is that the wrong people are going to have the wrong impact on you. It's important to surround yourself with positive, like-minded people when you want to grow and achieve the most in life.*

4. Determine to Live Differently than Average People

One of life's important questions is "Who am I?" But even more important is "Who am I becoming?" To answer that question, we must keep one eye on where we are and the other eye on where we want to be. Most people don't do that. They have one eye on where they have been and one eye on where they are now. That tells them who they have been. (And some people don't even examine themselves *that* much.) However, to know who you are becoming requires you not only to know where you are now but also to know where you're going and how you need to change to get there.

You've probably heard the statement "If you want something you've never had, you must do something you've never done." It's also true that if you want to become someone you have never been, you must do things you have never done. That means changing what you do every day. The secret to success can be found in your daily agenda. You have to put in the extra work every day to keep growing and changing.

JOURNAL IT!

Take some time to write in your journal what "average" effort would look like for you. Chances are, if you're reading this book, you already want to be above average. Write down what that means to you, too. Pay attention to the differences between the two descriptions. What kinds of changes will you need to make to get from where you are to where you want to be?

5. Unlearn What You Know to Learn What You Don't Know

Professional baseball pitcher Satchel Paige said, "It's not what you don't know that hurts you—it's what you do know that just ain't so." That is so true. Many things we learn are wrong, and we must unlearn them if we want to get better. Unlearning them can be difficult, but that is just another price we must pay if we want to grow.

Unlearning old or wrong ways of doing things can be difficult. We tend to lean on what we know, even if it's not the best for us. The secret is to allow yourself to be wrong and to be willing to change for the better. Psychiatrist David Burns says it this way: "Never give up your right to be wrong, because then you will lose the ability to learn new things and move forward with your life."

12

Maturity: The Value
of Learning

What do you get if you follow through with all the ideas I've been discussing in this book? Is there a pot of gold at the end of this rainbow? What happens if you:

Cultivate Humility: The Spirit of Learning

Face Reality: The Foundation of Learning

Accept Responsibility: The First Step of Learning

Seek Improvement: The Focus of Learning

Nurture Hope: The Motivation of Learning

Develop Teachability: The Pathway of Learning

Overcome Adversity: The Catalyst for Learning

Leverage Problems: The Opportunities for Learning

Endure Bad Experiences: The Perspective for Learning, and

Embrace Change: The Price of Learning

What happens if you do all of these things? You are rewarded with Maturity—The Value of Learning!

When I say *maturity*, I don't mean age. You don't have to be old to be mature. A mature person can learn from losses, understand the value of wisdom, and stay emotionally and mentally stable in the face of difficult situations. I have known mature sixteen-year-olds and immature fifty-six-year-olds.

Author William Saroyan observed, "Good people are good because they've come to wisdom through failure. We get very little wisdom from success, you know." What Saroyan is describing is this kind of maturity. To some, that quality comes at an early age. For others, it never comes.

Maturity is more often developed out of our losses than our wins. But *how* you face those losses really matters. People suffer losses, make mistakes, and endure bad experiences all the time without developing maturity. You have to have the right attitude.

Growing Pains

In chapter 11, I mentioned my dad's advice to always "pay now and play later." I heard that from him a lot while growing up. But it wasn't until I experienced a loss that I really grasped the lesson.

Like most parents, my mom and dad gave us kids chores

every week. They would usually give us the full week to complete the tasks. We could do them any day during that week. So we could complete them a little at a time, or put them off until the end of the week. But no matter what, they had to be done by noon on Saturday. Being the kind of kid that I was, who loved only to play, I usually put off my chores. Often, I was working at the last minute to meet my parents' deadline.

One week, my assignment was to clean out the basement. I was supposed to reorganize the workbench, rearrange boxes, and sweep everywhere. For a kid, that seemed like a huge task, so of course I put it off. Saturday morning, I still hadn't started, and my dad reminded me that it had to be done by noon. "Okay," I said. "I'll get it done."

Unfortunately, cleaning the basement was so big a task that I couldn't finish it in just a few hours, so when 12:00 came around, I was still working. That was when my dad came down to check on me. "Johnny, I see that you haven't finished your job," he said.

"I know, but I'm almost done," I replied, hoping I wouldn't get in too much trouble.

"Well, you keep working until you're done. But the rest of us are going to be gone the rest of the day. We're going swimming."

Swimming! Besides basketball, that was my favorite activity. And it was a hot summer day. I could only imagine how good that cold water would feel.

"Can't I come with you? I can finish after we get home," I said.

"No, son," he answered. "This is an example of 'pay now, play later.' You didn't pay on the front end, so you have to pay now. You won't be going swimming with us today."

Missing an afternoon of swimming might not seem like that big of a deal to you, but it was to me. That loss changed me. From then on, I determined to apply "pay now, play later" every day—to get the hard things done first, so that I could truly enjoy the fun later. I grew a little in maturity that day, by learning from a loss.

The Source of Maturity

If you desire to grow in maturity, then start taking the following steps:

1. Find the Benefit in the Loss

Learning from our mistakes is wonderful, but it means little if you don't know how to turn the lesson into a *benefit*. That comes when we take what we've learned and apply it to our future actions. When I decided to pay before playing, and then I actually did it, I was growing in maturity.

When I was young, I mistakenly thought that as I got older and gained experience, I would make fewer mistakes and suffer few losses. That hasn't been true. What I've discovered is that I still make mistakes and face losses, but I learn more quickly from them and am able to move on much more quickly on an emotional level.

If you want to gain the benefits learned from your losses and mistakes, don't allow them to take your attitude captive.

2. Feed the Right Emotions

Many years ago I came across a verse that I feel accurately describes the human condition. It says,

> *Two natures beat within my breast.*
> *The one is foul, the other blessed.*
> *The one I love, the other I hate,*
> *The one I feed will dominate.*[64]

I believe both positive and negative emotions are contained within each of us. There are people who teach that we should try to eliminate all negative feelings from our lives, but I have never been able to do that. I have tried, but I found that I simply can't. However, what I *can* do is feed the positive thoughts until they become stronger than the negative ones.

I try to feed the right emotions within myself by *acting* on the emotion that I want to win. "Do something every day that you don't want to do," advised author Mark Twain. "This is the golden rule for acquiring the habit of doing your duty without pain." Acting on the right emotion will lift you to success. Acting on the wrong emotion will lower you to failure.

> *Which emotions do you tend to feed? Do you spend your time and energy looking for the bright side, or do you allow yourself to focus on the negative, maybe complaining to your friends and family? Acting on the positive before you actually feel like it is the key. How can you take positive action today, in the face of your current circumstances?*

I once had lunch with Dom Capers, the successful NFL coach. One of the things he said during our conversation was, "Maturity is doing what you are supposed to be doing, when you're supposed to be doing it, no matter how you feel." That's true. The key to success is action. Too often we want to feel our way into action, when instead we need to act our way into feeling. If we do the right thing, we will eventually feel the right feelings.

3. Develop Good Habits

Og Mandino, author of *The Greatest Salesman in the World*, said, "In truth, the only difference between those who have failed and those who have succeeded lies in the difference of their habits." Through right actions, you encourage the right emotions. By doing that over and over, you can actually form the habit of taking the right action. And that often leads to further positive results.

Good habits require discipline and time to develop. When Benjamin Franklin was a young man, he decided to develop the habits he thought would improve him. Franklin listed thirteen qualities he desired to have, ranked them in order of importance, and then gave each its own page in a small notebook. He would concentrate on one quality each week, making notes in his little book. In time, he developed the qualities he admired, and it changed him from who he was to whom he desired to be.

People in high-pressure careers seem to learn this lesson early, or they don't reach the highest levels of success. For example, in professional ice skating, they call it "staying in your program." When a skater is doing a routine, if he or she makes a mistake or takes a fall, the skater is supposed to immediately get up and jump right back into the program— whether competing in the Olympics in front of hawk-eyed judges and millions of television watchers or practicing on his own in the early morning hours. It requires focus and the ability to live in the moment. Why is that important? Because to succeed at that high level, you can't allow a challenge to get you off track. You need to develop the habit of executing and following through.

If we want to gain the value of learning, we need to be in the habit of working at a high level, rain or shine, success or failure, setback or breakthrough.

4. Sacrifice Today to Succeed Tomorrow

I've touched on this point before, but it bears repeating. There is a definite connection between success and a person's willingness to make sacrifices. When I truly learned the "pay now, play later" lesson, I moved forward with the belief that putting off fun to do the hard work usually pays off in the end. The key is to remember that the good thing you're striving for will be better than the thing you're sacrificing.

Willingness to sacrifice does not come easily. People naturally tend to do things that make them feel good. Everyone likes comfort, pleasure, and entertainment, and they tend to want to keep experiencing them. If we keep doing this over and over, we can become either addicted or bored. Then we go after greater pleasures. For some people, this becomes a lifelong pursuit. But there's a problem with that. A person who cannot sacrifice will never belong to himself; he belongs to whatever he is unwilling to give up. If you want to develop maturity and gain the value of learning, you need to learn to give up some things today for greater gains tomorrow.

Q: How do I take my mind off the fun or easy route to focus on the big long-term goal?

A: As I've already mentioned, I love fun! Maturing in this area was hard for me. But over the years, I've discovered something that really helps me: creating some kind of visual reminder for myself. Sometimes it's a photo. Other times, it's a list of benefits. Or a statement of resolve that I can read aloud. Whatever it is, I put it where I'll see it every day, like on my bathroom mirror. That helps me stay on track when I'm tempted to veer off course.

5. Earn Respect for Yourself and from Others

Self-esteem is such a big deal today that I think some adults take it too far. Of course it's important for kids to feel good about themselves. But have you ever been around someone who felt *too good* about himself? Who was arrogant or lazy but expected people to praise him anyway? That's the downfall of emphasizing self-esteem too much. We adults praise kids so much for every little thing that some of them expect to be praised all the time. But that's not the real world.

People can tell you that you are wonderful all day long, whether you are or not, and it might make you feel good. But when you become an adult, not everyone will give you the same treatment.

The word *esteem* means "to appreciate the worth of, to hold in high regard, to have genuine respect." So *self-esteem* really means "self-respect." That comes from our character. We feel good about ourselves when we make right choices regardless of the circumstances. In fact, if our behavior is positive in the face of negative circumstances, it builds character and self-respect. This comes from inside each of us. And the better prepared we are to face our problems, the greater the maturity and the chance that we can learn and grow.

Author and speaker Brian Tracy says, "Self-esteem is the reputation you have with yourself." If you want it to be solid and lasting, it must be earned and confirmed, day by day. It happens from the inside out. And when it's solid, you know that external forces that come against you aren't going to shake it. You stay true to who you are to the core, you learn from your mistakes, and you keep moving forward.

Like I said earlier, maturity is not something that comes automatically with age. You can be thirteen and very mature in some areas, or you can be forty-three and still immature. By taking the time to read this book, you've already demonstrated a maturity that some adults never have. Instead, they live the way they always have, and are missing out on the knowledge that you've obtained. I hope you'll take what you've learned from these pages and apply it to your life today and every day. You have a great opportunity to start growing and learning from loss as a young adult. Just think of the course your life can take with this foundation! Turning losses into lessons will do more to help you mature than winning alone ever will. Make a habit of it, and you'll make huge strides on the journey of success.

13

Winning Isn't Everything, But Learning Is

I remember reading a *For Better or Worse* comic strip in which a boy is playing chess with his grandfather. "Oh, no! Not again!" cries the boy. "Grandpa, you always win!"

"What do you want me to do," answers his grandfather, "lose on purpose? You won't learn anything if I do that."

"I don't wanna learn anything," complains the boy. "I just wanna win!"

As well as anything I've ever seen, that captures how most of us feel. We just want to win! But the truth is that winning isn't everything—learning is.

Final Checklist

Author Douglas Adams said, "You live and learn. At any rate you live." It is possible to win and not learn. And for the person who puts winning ahead of learning, life will be difficult.

My purpose in writing this book has been to help you to discover how to learn—from your losses, failures, mistakes, challenges, and bad experiences. I want you to become a continual winner by being a habitual learner. To help you with that, here are some questions to ask yourself. Your answers will help guide you as you go forward.

1. Are You Ready to Believe That the More You Win, the Less You Learn?

Several years ago over dinner in Odessa, Texas, I had a conversation with Jim Collins, author of *Good to Great*. Jim is a good thinker, and I enjoy discussing leadership with him. At that time, the economy was going really well. We talked about how easy it is to get comfortable anytime people are winning. They are tempted to relax and sit back when things are going well. And Jim posed a question: "How do we continue to grow and improve and become more, when what we already have is pretty good?"

Complacency is a feeling of satisfaction with our successes. And that is the danger any person faces. Microsoft founder Bill Gates observed, "Success is a lousy teacher. It seduces smart people into thinking they can't lose." It also makes them think they don't need to learn.

The biggest danger to tomorrow's success is today's success. That problem can show itself in many ways. Here are the attitudes I've observed most often:

- *Been There, Done That:* Some people hit a milestone, and they make it a tombstone. They get bored, lose their curiosity, and disengage. They win the championship and start to think it was no big deal. Don't let that happen to you. Stay ambitious and focused.

- *The Awards Banquet:* When you succeed, people want to hear your story. However, there's a real danger that you can replace doing something with talking about what you've already done. When your team wins a championship, put the trophy on a shelf and get back to practice.

- *Success Guarantees Success:* Just because you can do one thing well doesn't mean you can do all things well. When you win, maintain your perspective and don't expect instant success in the future.

- *The Momentum Myth:* People's natural inclination after a win is to take a break. Bad idea. When you're winning, use that momentum. If you keep trying hard things, you'll be able to do things that might otherwise be impossible.

- *One-Hit Wonders:* Have you ever known someone who was successful *once*—and is still living off of it? It's a good idea to *build* off of yesterday; it's a bad idea to *live* off of it.

- *The Entitlement Mind-set:* People who have something that they didn't win for themselves start thinking they are entitled to more. That's why many inherited businesses go *out* of business. To keep winning, you need to stay hungry and keep learning.

- *Playing Not to Lose:* After some people win, they become cautious and defensive. They worry about staying on top. Not wanting to do something stupid, they do something stupid; they focus on not losing instead of on winning.
- *The Arrival Plateau:* Some people become so focused on a specific goal that when they hit it they give up, because they believe they've made it. That mind-set has the power to unmake them.

Any one of these wrong attitudes toward winning can turn a person from winner to loser very quickly. You've probably heard this phrase from a coach: "The number one rule of winning is don't beat yourself!" These are some of the most common ways people get off track once they've achieved some level of success.

If you want to keep learning and growing, you need to stay hungry. Depending on your personality, winning may remove some of your hunger to win again. So instead, keep your hunger to learn. Then no matter whether you win or lose, you'll keep getting better.

2. Are You Ready to Change Your Thinking?

Have you ever wondered why so many people who win the lottery lose all of their money? It happens all the time. One day they're holding a check worth millions, and a few years later they've lost it all. Why is that? The reason they lose their money is that they don't change their thinking. They may receive new money, but they hold on to their same old thinking about how to spend and save it. It's not what we have that determines our success. It's how we think. If they'd give up their thinking, then they might hold on to their money.

I've noticed three particular positive-thinking patterns of people who are always learning. Adopt them and you will be able to keep changing your thinking in a way to keep you learning:

Don't Let What You Know Make You Think That You Know Everything

Writer and philosopher J. Krishnamurti asserted, "To know is to be ignorant. Not to know is the beginning of wisdom." What does that mean? The only way to be wise is to first admit what you don't know. That's the only way you'll keep learning. It's easy when we're winning to begin to think we know everything. Don't let that happen! You simply can't learn what you think you already know.

You're still exploring as a young adult. I'm still exploring as an older adult. I know that I'm not close to knowing everything, and I don't think I ever will be. I believe that's what keeps me growing. If you can keep your beginner's mind-set, if you can remain teachable, you, too, can keep growing, even into old age.

Maintain a Positive Mental Attitude

I believe a key part of learning from loss comes from remaining positive. How do you do that? By continually feeding positive thoughts to your mind. Read positive books, listen to positive music, and hang out with positive people. When you do that, you supply your thinking with plenty of positive material, and you keep your mind focused on things that will encourage you.

When negative ideas and discouraging thoughts want to creep in and make you negative, you will have already created a barrier to them. Think positively long enough, and not only will your positive thoughts be stronger than your negative ones, they will be more comfortable, too.

Embrace Creativity in Every Situation

There's a classic brainteaser showing the power of creative thinking that I have sometimes shared with people when I teach. Here it is: using four straight lines, connect all nine dots below without crossing the same dot twice or lifting your pencil from the paper.

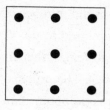

Did you solve it? Most people have a hard time with it the first time they try it. The secret is that you have to *go outside the box*! (If you're still not sure how to solve it, you can find the solution at the end of the chapter.)

Going outside the box is the key to much of the creative thinking that can help you to keep growing and learning. The problem is that most of us believe we are *supposed* to stay inside the box, remain inside the lines, and so forth. Who says so? There should be no restrictions to the way we think or how we approach problem solving. Wonderful, workable options are the rewards for becoming more creative.

3. Are You Ready to Change Your Behavior?

Humorist Will Rogers said, "There are three kinds of men. Ones that learn by reading, a few who learn by observation, and the rest of us have to pee on an electric fence and find out for ourselves." Ouch. That's got to hurt. But let's face it: some people only learn things the hard way.

The greatest gap in life is the one between knowing

and doing. I can't count the number of people I've met who *know* what they are supposed to do, yet don't take action on it. Sometimes it's due to fear. Other times to laziness. Other times to emotional issues. The problem is that knowing what to do and *not* doing it is no better than not knowing what to do. It ends in the same result: stagnation. You haven't really learned something until you've lived it. Or as poet Ralph Waldo Emerson said, "Life is a succession of lessons which must be lived to be understood."

4. Are You Ready to Continually Fail and Learn?

Chicago teacher Marva Collins says, "If you can't make a mistake, you can't make anything." How true. If you want to be successful, you must be willing to fail, and you must be intent on learning from those failures. If we are willing to repeat this fail-and-learn process, we become stronger and better than we were before.

Keep Taking Risks

As you move forward in life and work to achieve success, remember that progress requires risk, leads to failure, and provides many learning opportunities. Anytime you try something new, you must take a risk. That's just a part of learning.

When you take risks, you learn things faster than the people who don't take risks. You experiment. You learn more about what works and what doesn't. You overcome obstacles more quickly than the people who play it safe and are able to build on those experiences.

Political theorist Benjamin Barber said, "I divide the world into learners and nonlearners. There are people who learn, who are open to what happens around them, who listen, who hear the lessons. When they do something stupid, they don't do it again. And when they do something that works a little bit, they do it even better and harder the next time. The question to ask is not whether you are a success or a failure, but whether you are a learner or a nonlearner."

Keep Climbing

I don't know what your personal Mount Everest is— what you were put on this earth to do. Everybody has one. But I do know this: win or lose, you need to try to reach the summit. If you don't, you will always regret it. When you're older, you will be more disappointed by the things you didn't attempt than by the ones you tried and failed to achieve. And here's the best news: every step of the way there's something to learn. Even after you graduate from school, you are enrolled in a full-time informal school called life. In it, there are no mistakes, only lessons. Growth is a process of trial and error, experimentation and improvement. The failed experiments are as much of that process as the ones that work.

The lessons you have the opportunity to learn will be presented to you in various forms. Fail to learn the lesson and you get stuck, unable to move forward. Learn the lesson and you get to move forward and go to the next one. And if you do it right, the process never ends. There is no part of life that doesn't contain lessons. If you're alive, that means you still have opportunities ahead of you to learn. You just have to be willing to tackle them. You have all the tools and resources you need. The choice is yours. Others will give you advice. Some may even help you. But you have to take the test. Sometimes you will win. Sometimes you will lose. But every time you will have the opportunity to ask yourself, "What did I learn?" If you always have an answer to that question, then you will go far. And you will enjoy the journey.

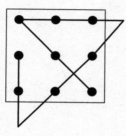

Notes

1. Kirk Hanson, university professor and executive director of the Markkula Center for Applied Ethics at Santa Clara University, offers a list of characteristics exhibited by unteachable leaders.
2. "John Wooden: Life and Times," UCLA, http://www.spotlight.ucla.edu/john-wooden/life-and-times/, accessed September 23, 2010.
3. John Wooden and Don Yeager, *A Game Plan for Life: The Power of Mentoring* (New York: Bloomsbury, 2009), 34.
4. Charlotte Foltz Jones, *Mistakes That Worked* (New York: Doubleday, 1991), 8–9.
5. Chris Dufresne, "Sochi Olympics: Mikaela Shiffrin Overcomes Near Crash to Win Gold," *Los Angeles Times*, February 21, 2014, http://articles.latimes.com/2014/feb/21/sports/la-sp-sochi-womens-slalom-20140222, accessed May 2, 2014.
6. Bill Pennington, "In Slalom, Mikaela Shiffrin Zips to Bottom and Reaches the Pinnacle," *New York Times*, February 21, 2014, http://www.nytimes.com/2014/02/22/sports/olympics/american-mikaela-shiffrin-wins-gold-in-slalom.html?_r=2, accessed May 2, 2014.
7. Charlene Schiff, "Charlene Schiff: A Daughter's Separation from Her Mother," First Person Podcast Series (transcript), United States Holocaust Memorial Museum, http://www.ushmm.org/information/museum-programs-and-calendar/first-person-program/first-person-podcast/charlene-schiff-a-daughters-separation-from-her-mother, accessed July 17, 2014.
8. Charlene Schiff as told to Sam Boykin, in "Home of the Brave," *Reader's Digest*, April 2009, 149.

9. "Charlene Schiff (Shulamit Perlmutter)," Survivor Volunteers, United States Holocaust Memorial Museum, http://www.ushmm.org/remember/office-of-survivor-affairs/survivor-volunteer/charlene-schiff, accessed July 17, 2014.

10. "Charlene Schiff: A Daughter's Separation."

11. "Charlene Schiff (Shulamit Perlmutter)."

12. Ibid.

13. Boykin, "Home of the Brave."

14. Ibid.

15. "The Comeback Kid" *The Oprah Winfrey Show* (video), November 23, 2004, http://www.oprah.com/oprahshow/The-Comeback-Kid, accessed May 1, 2014.

16. Mike Zimmerman, "The Business of Being Robert Downey, Jr.," *Success*, http://www.success.com/article/the-business-of-being-robert-downey-jr, accessed May 1, 2014.

17. Frances Cole Jones, *The Wow Factor: The 33 Things You Must (and Must Not) Do to Guarantee Your Edge in Today's Business World* (New York: Ballantine Books, 2009), 30–31.

18. Tony Rossi, "Grace, Gold and Glory: An Interview with Olympic Gold Medalist Gabrielle Douglas and Her Mom, Natalie Hawkins," *Patheos*, April 17, 2013, http://www.patheos.com/blogs/christophers/2013/04/grace-gold-glory-an-interview-with-olympic-gold-medalist-gabrielle-douglas-and-her-mom-natalie-hawkins/, accessed May 6, 2014.

19. Alice Park, "History-Making High: How U.S. Gymnast Gabrielle Douglas Became the Olympic All-Around Champion," *Time*, August 2, 2012, http://olympics.time.com/2012/08/02/history-making-high-how-u-s-gymnast-gabrielle-douglas-became-the-olympic-all-around-champion/, accessed May 6, 2014.

20. Bethany Hamilton, *Soul Surfer* (New York: Pocket Books, 2004), 105.

21. Ibid., 179.

22. Tom Hamilton, "The Fire and Faith in Her Eyes," *Guideposts*, http://www.guideposts.org/hope-and-faith/surfer-bethany-hamilton-has-strong-faith-after-shark-attack?page=full, accessed May 10, 2014.

23. Aaron Lieber, "Bethany Hamilton: How Does She Do It?" (video), available at http://www.surfline.com/surflinetv/featured-clips/bethany-hamilton-how-does-she-do-it_107855, accessed May 10, 2014.

24. Ibid.

25. "About," Friends of Bethany, http://www.friendsofbethany.com/about/.

26. Marie Speed, "Your Personal Best: Bethany Hamilton Is Back on the Board," *Success*, http://www.success.com/article/your-personal-best-bethany-hamilton-is-back-on-the-board, accessed May 10, 2014.

27. Jonathan Sacks, *The Dignity of Difference: How to Avoid the Clash of Civilizations* (New York: Continuum, 2002), 206.

28. Jim Abbott and Tim Brown, *Imperfect: An Improbable Life* (New York: Ballantine Books, 2012), 55.

29. Ibid., 56.

30. Ibid., 58.

31. Ibid., 61.

32. Ibid., 66.

33. Ibid., 182.

34. Ibid., 183.

35. "Jim Abbott Career Stats," MLB.com, http://mlb.mlb.com/team/player .jsp?player_id=110009, accessed September 10, 2012.

36. Abbott and Brown, *Imperfect*, 276.

37. Josh Waitzkin, *The Art of Learning* (New York: Free Press, 2007), xii.

38. "About Josh," Josh Waitzkin—Official Website, http://joshwaitzkin .com/#!about-josh.

39. Waitzkin, *The Art of Learning*, xix.

40. Ibid., 108.

41. Hal Urban, *Life's Greatest Lessons: 20 Things That Matter* (New York: Fireside, 2003), 40.

42. Michael Oher, *I Beat the Odds* (New York: Gotham Books, 2011), 51.

43. Ibid., 21.

44. Ibid., 89.

45. Ibid.

46. Ibid., 129.

47. Michael Lewis, "The Ballad of Big Mike," *New York Times Magazine*, September 24, 2006, http://www.nytimes.com/2006/09/24/magazine/ 24football.html, accessed June 22, 2014.

48. Oher, *I Beat the Odds*, 189.

49. Barbara Chai, "Listen to Songs from Disney's 'Frozen' and Hear How They Were Written," *Speakeasy* (blog), *Wall Street Journal,* November 27, 2013, http://blogs.wsj.com/speakeasy/2013/11/27/listen-to-songs-from -disneys-frozen-and-hear-how-they-were-written/, accessed July 9, 2014.

50. Laura Ferreiro, "Demi Lovato's Triumph over Tragedy, and How She 'Let It Go,'" *Yahoo! Music*, April 10, 2014, https://music.yahoo.com/blogs/ yahoo-music/demi-lovato-triumph-over-tragedy-she-let-185213608.html, accessed July 9, 2014.

51. Robert H. Schuller, *Tough Times Never Last, But Tough People Do!* (New York: Bantam Books, 1984), 73.

52. *Understanding the Winds of Adversity*, Supplementary Alumni Book, vol- ume 7 (Oak Brook, IL: Institute in Basic Youth Conflicts, 1981), quoted

in Bill Scheidler, "Understanding Suffering and Affliction," Church LeadershipResources.com, http://www.churchleadershipresources.com/DownloadLanding.aspx?resourceId=2662&openOrSave=Save, accessed September 28, 2012.

53. Malala Yousafzai with Christina Lamb, *I Am Malala* (New York: Little, Brown, 2013), 232.

54. Mishal Husain, "Malala: The Girl Who Was Shot for Going to School," *BBC News Magazine*, October 7, 2013, http://www.bbc.com/news/magazine-24379018, accessed May 10, 2014.

55. Ashley Fantz, "Malala at U.N.: The Taliban Failed to Silence Us," CNN World, http://www.cnn.com/2013/07/12/world/united-nations-malala/index.html, accessed May 10, 2014.

56. http://malalafund.org/.

57. Husain, "Malala: The Girl Who Was Shot for Going to School."

58. Pat Forde, "U.S. Olympic Swim Trials are Exhilarating for Top Two Finishers, Excruciating If You End Up Third," *Yahoo! Sports*, June 24, 2012, http://sports.yahoo.com/news/olympics--u-s--olympic-swim-trials-excruciating-if-you-finish-third.html, accessed October 1, 2012.

59. "Smartphone Milestone: Half Of Mobile Subscribers Ages 55+ Own Smartphones," Nielsen Newswire, April 22, 2014, http://www.nielsen.com/us/en/newswire/2014/smartphone-milestone-half-of-americans-ages-55-own-smartphones.html, accessed May 12, 2014.

60. Brian Williams, "Steve Jobs: Iconoclast and Salesman," *NBC Nightly News with Brian Williams*, May 25, 2006, http://www.nbcnews.com/id/12974884/#.U3D80a1dUr4, accessed May 12, 2014.

61. Josh Tyrangiel, "Tim Cook's Freshman Year: The Apple CEO Speaks," *Business Week*, December 6, 2012, http://www.businessweek.com/articles/2012-12-06/tim-cooks-freshman-year-the-apple-ceo-speaks, accessed May 12, 2014.

62. Maria Popova, "The Secret of Life from Steve Jobs in 46 Seconds," Brain Pickings, December 2, 2011, http://www.brainpickings.org/index.php/2011/12/02/steve-jobs-1995-life-failure/, accessed May 12, 2014.

63. Fred Vogelstein, "And Then Steve Said, 'Let There Be an iPhone,'" *New York Times Magazine*, October 4, 2013, http://www.nytimes.com/2013/10/06/magazine/and-then-steve-said-let-there-be-an-iphone.html?_r=0, accessed May 12, 2014.

64. Author unknown.

About the Author

John C. Maxwell is a number one *New York Times* bestselling author, coach, and speaker who has sold more than 24 million books in fifty languages. Often called America's number one leadership authority, Maxwell was identified as the most popular leadership expert in the world by *Inc.* magazine in 2014. And he has been voted the top leadership professional six years in a row on LeadershipGurus.net. He is the founder of the John Maxwell Company, the John Maxwell Team, and EQUIP, a nonprofit organization that has trained more than 5 million leaders in 180 countries. Each year, Maxwell speaks to Fortune 500 companies, presidents of nations, and many of the world's top business leaders. He can be followed at Twitter.com/JohnCMaxwell. For more information about him visit JohnMaxwell.com.

How Successful People Grow:
15 Ways to Get Ahead in Life

Want to become the person you were
created to be? John Maxwell shows you
how by doing fifteen things anyone
can do.

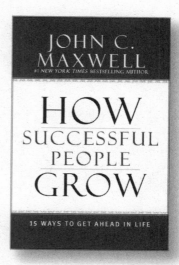

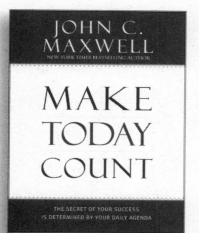

Make Today Count: The Secret
of Your Success Is Determined
by Your Daily Agenda

Twelve daily practices can help you
make the most of today and every day.

How Successful People Think:
Change Your Thinking, Change
Your Life

Maxwell reveals eleven types of thinking
all successful people do. Learn them and
how they can help you succeed in all
aspects of your life.

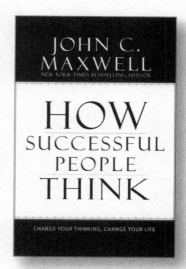